Quotable Chicago

By the Same Author

Stuck on the Sox (1978)

Who's on Third? The Chicago White Sox Story (1983)

The Macmillan White Sox Encyclopedia (1984)

Chicago Ragtime: Another Look at Chicago 1880–1920 (1985)

To Serve and Collect: Chicago Politics and Police Corruption from the Lager Beer Riot to the Summerdale Scandal (1991)

Passport's Guide to Ethnic Chicago (1992)

Stealing First in a Two Team Town: The White Sox from Comiskey to Reinsdorf (1994)

Chicago by Gaslight: A History of Chicago's Netherworld, 1880–1920 (1996)

Contributing Writer

A Kid's Guide to Chicago (1980)

The Encyclopedia of Major League Team Histories (1989)

The Encyclopedia of World Crime (1990)

The Baseball Biographical Encyclopedia (1990)

American National Biography (1997 revision series)

Quotable
Chicago

Richard C. Lindberg

Wild Onion Books

an imprint of Loyola Press

Chicago

∞

Wild Onion Books
an imprint of Loyola Press
3441 North Ashland Avenue
Chicago, Illinois 60657

Wild Onion Books publishes provocative titles on Chicago themes that offer diverse perspectives on the city and surrounding area, its history, its culture, and its religions. Wild onion is a common nickname for Chicago.

Wild Onion Books staff:
Imprint editors: June Sawyers, Jeremy Langford
Interior design and production coordination: Jill Mark Salyards

Cover direction: Frederick O. Falkenberg
Cover design: Tammi Longsjo

Studs Terkel quotes are from his book *Talking to Myself,* Pantheon, 1977.

Library of Congress Cataloging-in-Publication Data
Lindberg, Richard, 1953—
    Quotable Chicago / Richard C. Lindberg.
        p.   cm.
    ISBN 0-8294-0927-0
    1. Chicago (Ill.)—Quotation, maxims, etc.   I. Title
F548.52.L56   1996
977.3'11—dc20
96 97 98 99 00 / 6 5 4 3 2

96-24502
CIP

To my fellow Merry Gangsters,
Bill Reilly and Nate Kaplan, in memorial.

Contents

■ ■ ■

Foreword by Bill Granger	*xi*
Acknowledgments	*xiii*
Introduction	*xv*
Notes on Chicago Quotes	*xxv*
1. As the World Sees Us	1
2. Empire of the Prairie	27
3. Money Talks	55
4. Acid Ink and Poison Pens	73
5. Athletes' Feats	91
6. Crime and Punishment	109
7. Clout City	123
8. Our Daley Bread	147
9. Uplifting Voices	159
10. The Social Conscience of a City	173
11. Meet the Press	191
12. Performing Arts	203
Index	221

Foreword

■ ■ ■

Everything said memorably in Chicago was short and sweet.

So it seems in Rich Lindberg's new book of quotes.

The selection is as arbitrary as an alderman issuing a zoning variance. So much the better. It can start fights. Nothing better than a fight over a stupid point. Sort of like White Sox and Cubs fans explaining why their team isn't nearly as terrible as the other guy's team.

Chicago talk is never misunderstood, even when it is absurd. Brevity makes its own point for it. Mayor Richard M. Daley, Son of Himself, said, "Everybody's worried about apathy." Absurd on the face of it as quoted in this book—but quite plain in its meaning. As his father once said, "Together, we must rise to ever higher and higher platitudes." Press quotations of Himself once led his faithful press secretary, Earl Bush, to tell reporters: "Write what he means, not what he says." It couldn't have been sung better.

And there are singers quoted in this book, singers of street songs. Like Nelson Algren, who made poetry even when he fumbled over the typewriter keys after a few drinks:

"Loving Chicago is like loving a woman with a broken nose."

Or Carl Sandburg, who did the Hog Butcher thing when he was feeling real poetic, but let down his white hair when he spoke some Chicago nitty-gritty: "Here's the difference between us and Dante. He wrote a lot about hell and never saw the place. We're writing about Chicago after looking the town over."

This book is too brief, a Chicago conversation that takes place on a windy street corner in January. But it gets to the point.

Fun read.

—Bill Granger

Acknowledgments

■ ■ ■

This treasury of quotes could not have been possible without the help of the staff of the Chicago Historical Society library who have graciously assisted me in my research endeavors over the years—Emily Clark, Patrick Ashley, Tim Hagan, and Jan McNeill. Also, a tip of the hat to the Deckerts—Frank, Ellen, Anna, and Frank James—Sandy Roth, John Binder, Trudy Wallace, Frank Sullivan, Jim Agnew, Pat Fulton, Wayne Anderson, Denise Lindberg, Patrick Flynn, Bill Granger, Barbara Schaaf, Frankie Laine, Studs Terkel, Rose Keefe, Bill Helmer, June Sawyers, and Jeremy Langford of Loyola Press—Chicagoans all (well, almost), who love the Windy City unconditionally.

Introduction

■ ■ ■

To love a city is to delight in the beauty of its most spacious boulevards and its sooty back alleys. Within a visual mélange of endless contradictions that elevate the senses and stimulate our thought processes come a more human element.

There is much more to Chicago than thick-crust pizza, great jazz, and Michael Jeffrey Jordan's nightly ballet on the hardwood. There is also a human drama, eloquently expressed in the spoken and printed word that we have tried to capture in this volume of quotations, writings, and personal reminiscences.

This is a city caught up in its lusty past; a town that pulsates to a rhythmic, sometimes somber, beat played out in the corner taverns, the church parishes, the public parks, or wherever people gather to share a sense of community and to better understand themselves.

The historical strength of any city rests in the soul of its people who dwell in the neighborhoods, and from its earliest days Chicago has evoked a restless spirit that has challenged its newcomers to scale the heights in the leanest of times and toughest of circumstances.

Once there stood a bustling city on the edge of a majestic lakefront that was knocked flat in one flaming, harrowing night—but whose citizens chose not to dwell in the useless exercise of self-pity. Their heroic effort to rebuild this great city from the twisted metal, broken shards of glass, and smoking debris of the Chicago Fire of 1871 was an expression of a profound belief in the unlimited future of humankind, approaching the dawn of the century. Entrepreneurs of solid New England stock, unencumbered by hardships, great and small, forged an empire on the prairie in the decades following the Civil War.

Nineteenth-century Chicago was a city of hustlers, visionaries, and entrepreneurs who washed up on its marshy banks for the avowed purpose of making money as fast and as unscrupulously as they could. The makers and rulers of empire established this once desolate frontier outpost at the confluence of the Chicago River and Lake Michigan as the regional hub of Midwestern commerce. Real estate speculators, builders, and architects fueled by energy and imagination were quick to realize Chicago's enormous potential. The Illinois and Michigan Canal opened in 1848, and with it came the portals of commerce from the river towns dotting the mighty Mississippi River. Later still came the steel-frame skyscraper and the emergence of the modern city. Chicago was not a place for the timid or fainthearted.

Parcels of valuable downtown land, once the property of the native Potawatomi, who were forced to relinquish their claims for trifling sums of money and driven further west by the government, were bought up by shrewd pioneer speculators such as John Kinzie and William B. Ogden, Chicago's first mayor. A town on the edge of the ragged frontier arose from the muck and mire of the wet flatlands surrounding the blockhouses of old Fort Dearborn, where the troops were once garrisoned. Chicagoans were knee-deep in mud, and cholera was a constant threat to the populace until these imaginative thinkers elevated the city street five feet in the air.

Vast fortunes were quickly accumulated by men who erected gaudy Victorian palaces on Prairie Avenue—the boulevard of millionaires in the waning years of the old century. The Fields, MacVeighs, Palmers, McCormicks, Pullmans, Armours, and Swifts subscribed to a nineteenth-century paradigm of self-reliance and social Darwinism that casually disregarded

society's have-nots, except when it came time to hire the newly
arrived domestic help, the footmen, and the masons.

Their luxurious palaces frequently were staffed with immigrant Irish cooks and maids, and a fleet of elegantly
appointed carriages were manufactured by the Kimball Company at Harrison and Wabash in the futile hope of imitating
the trappings of New York society, whose arbiters of social
taste had dismissed Chicago as a rather vulgar and showy
place with no appreciation for art, music, and good breeding.

In the rush to acquire money, prestige, and social title,
Chicago's blue-blooded entrepreneurs who built their palatial
and extravagant estates along Prairie Avenue, Grand Boulevard,
and the emerging Gold Coast north of the Chicago River,
ignored the swirling social changes taking place around them.
Beginning in the 1880s and continuing without interruption
until the mid-1920s, thousands of dirt-poor immigrants, possessing little more than tattered rags on their backs and an abiding
faith in the promise of America, poured into the central city.

Chicago tapped its greatest strength not from the drawing
rooms of Prairie Avenue aristocrats but from the plain people,
whose toil, self-sacrifice, and confidence in the future tamed a
wild frontier. It was a lean, spartan existence. Infant mortality
was high, and the workingmen and -women had little
recourse other than to accept substandard wages and the

squalor of unheated wooden shacks on the periphery of the downtown business district.

The oppressed, as they do often do, cried out against inhumanity and social injustice. A bloody strike at the McCormick Reaper Works culminated in the Haymarket Riot of May 4, 1886, and a fire bell in the night awakened organized labor, tenuous and uncertain of its direction in the years leading up to the tragedy, to rally behind the eight-hour movement that took shape in Chicago and was championed by the eight anarchists who were ultimately held accountable for the deaths of the eight police officers, ~~blown to bits when the~~ Haymarket bomb suddenly and without warning fell ~~within their ranks~~ that dark and drizzly May night. Haymarket. A Chicago event with worldwide repercussions.

[handwritten annotation: PROBABLY KILLED BY FRIENDLY FIRE]
[handwritten annotation: AFTER THE Haymarket bomb ... fell ON THE STREET]

Chicago's uplifting voices stirred the conscience of the city. The four Haymarket martyrs, who stood upon the gallows a year after the bomb, altered the course of labor history, shaped the thinking, and set the directions for future generations of idealists and thinkers seeking to counterbalance the frenzy to accumulate fortunes in the grain pits and South Side stockyards with the needs and wants of the poor. Saul Alinsky, Emma Goldman, Sidney Hillman, and Jane Addams, shaken by the Haymarket tragedy, became among the most eloquent spokespersons for the downtrodden and the despairing.

Haymarket, the eight-hour movement, and the Pullman Strike, occurring eight years after the fateful bombing, foreshadowed a renaissance in urban expression that beckoned to Chicago the brightest and most creative voices of the Midwestern prairie. Within its dark landscapes, Theodore Dreiser, Carl Sandburg, Sherwood Anderson, Harriet Monroe, Ring Lardner, James T. Farrell, Margaret Anderson, and Finley Peter Dunne (whose homespun but sage philosophy was best articulated through his fictional South Side Irish barkeep, Martin Dooley), tapped the source of their greatest inspiration. For a brief and shining moment, Chicago had become all that it prophesied in its motto—*Urbs in Horto*—the City in a Garden.

Viewed historically, the city aspired to the highest ideals of humankind while often pandering to the baser elements of human existence. Taking author Robert Casey at his word, "Chicago is an independent miracle; vigorous, powerful, and uninhibited."

By the 1920s, around the time the last of a generation of writers, poets, and painters pronounced the last rites on a literary renaissance that temporarily elevated the city out of the muck and graft of the late 1880s and early 1890s, the City in a Garden returned to its familiar boodling ways and had again evolved into Clout City, a dreary manifestation of the sinister forces of corrupt aldermen in league with the legions of gangsters, bagmen, and influence peddlers of deal-cutting, hustling, fast-buck Chicago.

Writing for *McClure's* magazine, muckraking journalist Lincoln Steffens held out few hopes for the large urban centers caught in the chokehold of saloon-bred ward bosses and the imposing political machines they served. "Political corruption . . . is not a passing symptom of the youth of a people. It is the natural process by which a democracy is made gradually over to a plutocracy." And with it came a reputation for urban deception and chicanery that lingers to this day.

The modern city of Chicago is a reflection of this historical evolution, and its citizens seem to take a perverse and cynical pride in the international notoriety of its gangsters, reveling in the details of the latest "one-way ride" and the magnitude of the dishonesty of its elected officials. We may be the Second City in spirit, but no urban center other than Chicago could claim Al Capone as its most favored son. Some are even proud of that legacy. Let no one tell you differently.

In the long run, politics and money is what it's all about. It is the synthesis of Chicago and one of the reasons why we have hosted more national nominating conventions than any other city. The legendary Democratic political machine that emerged in the 1930s under Anton Cermak and the stewardships of Edward Kelly and Martin Kennelly became a cattle driver that politicized average workaday Chicagoans and prodded them into the polling place on Election Day to pull the magical lever that perpetuated their jobs, their livelihood.

It was entirely appropriate that an Irish-American family from Bridgeport—Chicago's oldest and most historic ethnic settlement—should come to control the destiny of the city, forge the longest-running political dynasty in American history, and leave behind a collection of some of the most colorful and unintentionally hilarious quotations and anecdotes the city has heard in many a year. Richard J. Daley, a devout Catholic and family man, elevated the Chicago Democratic machine to legendary heights. "Hizzoner," the mayor, was not an articulate man (and neither is his son Richard M., unfortunately), but together they cast a long, indomitable shadow across the land. For decades, Daley the elder, in particular, was a potent blend of statesmanship and political wheeler-dealing. If not for the influence (shenanigans?) of the elder Daley in his traditional Democratic strongholds, Richard Nixon, not John F. Kennedy, surely would have been elected president in 1960.

Majestic new skyscrapers, a stately convention hall, a ribbon of expressways, and a state-of-the-art airport that cemented Chicago's place as one of the most important transportation hubs of the world in the 1960s highlighted the first Daley regime. Heads of state, visiting dignitaries of every stripe, and astronauts—Mayor Daley was an enthusiastic supporter of the space program—paid their homage to the "City That Works" throughout the 1950s, 1960s, and 1970s. Dick Daley, his roots grounded in the broken pavement of old Bridgeport, with its saloons, parishes, shabby storefronts, and modest brick bungalows, truly enjoyed his role as a big-city mayor, showing off his kind of town to the world while encouraging some of Chicago's homegrown latter-day entrepreneurs to build and prosper. But even before Daley, the Windy City was an important stopover point for those desiring to learn the essential truths about the American character.

From its earliest days, Chicago has thrown its husky, broad arms around visiting celebrities in the spirit of friendship— dating back to 1860, when the youthful prince of Wales was shown the lay of the land by Mayor John Wentworth. Chicago—as the world sees us—illustrates a great paradox.

The Irish poet Oscar Wilde was critical of Chicago during his celebrated 1882 American tour. The ~~effeminate~~ Oscar, the first important literary figure to grace our shore, found much to criticize in local architecture and social customs, and he publicly fumed over the seat-of-the-pants criticism heaped upon him by a rough-hewn press corps, weaned, as it was, on whiskey, a healthy appreciation for the ludicrously absurd, and a suspicion of outsiders "puttin' on airs."

The youthful, extremely self-conscious city bowed and scraped to Wilde and bent over backwards to impart a favorable impression—one they hoped he might take with him to the European capitals. But if Chicago society counted on Oscar Wilde to sing the artistic praises of the city and its budding aesthetic refinements, they were sadly disappointed.

Others, like H. G. Wells and Rudyard Kipling, recognized that the thriving city was a living, breathing entity—the sum total of its parts. "I have struck a real city," Kipling later wrote. And so it would be, down to the time of the two Daleys.

Our visitors may have uncovered distasteful elements within the urban fabric—slums, urban blight, public corruption—but rarely did they leave disappointed or bored by what they had seen. Like Kipling, they indeed had struck a *real* city.

This is the essence of the windy burg situated on a prairie—a raw, uninhibited dynamo; a metropolis possessing the arrogance of its conviction to boldly declare, "I Will." Or, to paraphrase the words of the Emperor Napoleon, we lend dignity to what otherwise would be a dull affair.

Now, may I present to you the unvarnished Chicago—in its own words.

Notes on Chicago Quotes

■ ■ ■

It is impossible to authenticate some of the attributed quotes contained in this volume. The passage of time and the possibility that the actual words were twisted by reporters who were eager to spice up a slow news day present an eternal dilemma for the chronicler of the spoken word. In the rush to create compelling human-interest drama in the tabloids, some of our most famous and enduring quotes probably were never spoken at all. With apologies to "Shoeless" Joe Jackson, one of the tragic figures of the 1919 Black Sox scandal, "Say it ain't so, Joe," was in all likelihood the figment of the overactive imagination of a zealous newspaper rewrite man.

Was it 1870s Chicago gambling boss Mike McDonald or "Texas" Guinan, the gin-soaked Jazz Age maven, who reminded us that "there's a sucker born every minute"? Maybe we will never find out, but Chicago has produced its own unique breed of suckers, gamblers, grifters, priests, and poets with something interesting to say.

However, we can state with no equivocation that Alderman Mathias "Paddy" Bauler of the Forty-Third Ward did indeed utter the city's most recognizable quote, "Chicago ain't ready for reform," the night Mayor Richard J. Daley was elected to his first term of office in 1955. We know this to be true because we have it on good word from some of the old reliables who lived through the rough-and-tumble saloon era of Chicago politics.

Bauler owned Chicago's most famous watering hole from 1933 until he shut the lights off in 1960. For years it was the favorite gathering spot for the pols, the crooks, and the cops, especially on Election Day and Saint Patrick's Day, when the genial host donned his silken top hat and hoisted the largest schooner of lager seen in these parts since "Hinky Dink" Kenna's time.

Bauler's legendary quote struck a raw nerve in a town desperately fighting to live down the history of its reputation. The *Chicago Sun-Times* bristled in righteous indignation in the pages of their editorial section the very next day.

After all these years Chicago is still not ready for reform and probably never will be, but the famous one-liners will surely keep coming, and we will be there to record them as fast as they are spoken.

1

As the
World Sees Us

We have seen nothing like this river we enter as regards its fertility of soil, its prairies and woods; its cattle, elk, deer, wildcats, bustards, swans, ducks, parroquets, and even beaver.

> FATHER JACQUES MARQUETTE,
> *crossing the Chicago portage*
> *on the Illinois River, 1673*

And my people who, having marched three days along the lake and gained the portage called Chicagou, were waiting . . . the land there produces naturally a quantity of roots good to eat as wild ognons [onions].

> RENÉ-ROBERT CAVELIER SIEUR DE LA SALLE,
> *French voyageur's final expedition*
> *into the Mississippi Valley, 1681*

The population of Chicago is said to be principally composed of dogs and loafers.

> *Jackson, Michigan,*
> *newspaper comment, 1839*

It is a remarkable thing to meet such an assemblage of educated, refined, and wealthy persons as may be found there, living in small, inconvenient houses on the edge of the wind prairie.

> HARRIET MARTINEAU, *lecturer,*
> *author, radical Victorian, 1840*

In ten years Chicago will be as big as Albany.

> THURLOW WEED,
> *New York journalist, 1847*

Chicago is one of the most miserable and ugly cities which I have yet seen in America, and is very little deserving of its name "Queen of the Lake"; for, sitting there on the shore of the lake, she is wretched, dishabille. She resembles rather a huckstress than a queen.

> FREDERIKA BREMER, *Swedish novelist, 1853*

I wish I could go to America if only to see that Chicago.

> OTTO VON BISMARCK,
> *German chancellor, 1870*

Chicago is almost as great a city for worldliness and wickedness as for trade. What she does she does with all her might. Her good people are very good, her bad people are very bad. Everything works at high pressure. The first thing that strikes a stranger is the universal rush for wealth.

> DAVID MACRAE, *Scottish visitor,*
> The Americans at Home, *1870*

Gentlemen of the Board of Trade, I take great pleasure in introducing to you the king of the Cannibal Islands!

> HARVEY DOOLITTLE COLVIN, *mayor*
> *of Chicago, 1873–76, introducing*
> *the king of the Sandwich Islands*
> *to the business community*

Chicago, if not *the* most cruel city, is certainly *one* of the most cruel cities in the world.

> GEORGE THORNDIKE ANGELL, *founder of the Society for the Prevention of Cruelty to Animals, 1870*

Queen of the West!
By some enchanter taught
To lift the glory of Aladdin's court
Then lose the spell that all that wonder wrought,
Like her own prairies by some chance seed sown,
Like her own prairies in one brief day grown,
Like her own prairies in one fierce night mown.

> BRET HARTE, *novelist and poet, "Chicago," 1871*

I adore Chicago. It is the pulse of America.

> SARAH BERNHARDT, *nineteenth-century French actress*

Chicago sounds rough to the maker of verse. One comfort we have—Cincinnati sounds worse.

OLIVER WENDELL HOLMES, *January 1880*

Your machinery is beautiful. Your society people have apologized to me for the envious ridicule with which your newspapers have referred to me. Your newspapers are comic but never amusing. Your Water Tower is a castellated monstrosity with pepperboxes stuck all over it. I am amazed that any people could so abuse Gothic art and make a structure not like a water tower but like a tower of a medieval castle. It should be torn down. It is a shame to spend so much money on buildings with such an unsatisfactory result. Your city looks positively dreary.

OSCAR WILDE, *Irish poet, critic, and dandy, February 13, 1882*

Chicago is a nice place, but I wouldn't want to live there.

HARLOW KIMBALL, *1883*

We struck the home trail now, and in a few hours we're in that astonishing Chicago—a city where they are always rubbing the lamp and fetching up the genii and contriving and achieving new impossibilities. It is hopeless for the occasional visitor to try to keep up with Chicago—she outgrows his prophecies faster than he can make them. She is always a novelty; for she is never the Chicago you saw when you passed through the last time.

MARK TWAIN, Life on the Mississippi, *1883*

I have struck a city—a real city. And they call it Chicago. The other places do not count.

RUDYARD KIPLING, *English author,*
From Sea to Sea, *a report of
Kipling's travels abroad, 1887–89*

Chicago is a comparatively enlightened town. My plays get good houses there.

GEORGE BERNARD SHAW, *1900*

We in New York are familiar with the sharp character of the Chicago magnates, and many of us have learned that the almighty dollar is the trail they are following. These Chicagoans should not pretend to rival the East or the Old World in matters and refinement.

> WARD MCALLISTER, *nineteenth-century*
> *social critic, c. 1892*

Chicago, great in executing enterprises which can be executed under the stress and strain of a strong stimulus, is not equally great in preserving and maintaining that which she has created.

> WILLIAM T. STEAD, *English reformer, c. 1895*

Chicago likes audacity and is always willing to try something once; no matter who you are, where you come from, or what you set out to do, Chicago will give you a chance.

> LINCOLN STEFFENS, *turn-of-the century*
> *journalist and muckraker, c. 1900*

If you can't make it here, you can't make it anywhere.

Old Chicago proverb from bygone days

The heart and center of Chicago is the huge pile of masonry which reminds the visitor by its polished granite pillars and general massive and somber grandeur of the cathedrals and palaces of St. Petersburg.

WILLIAM T. STEAD,
If Christ Came to Chicago, *1894*

Chicago! Chicago, queen and guttersnipe of cities, cynosure and cesspool of the world! Not if I had a hundred tongues, every one shouting a different language in a different key, would I do justice to her splendid chaos.

GEORGE STEEVENS,
London Daily Mail, *1896*

First in violence, deepest in dirt, lawless, unlovely, ill-smelling, irreverent, new. An over-grown gawk of a village—the "tough" among cities, a spectacle for the nation.

LINCOLN STEFFENS,
The Shame of the Cities, *1905*

One reason for knowing the history of Chicago is that the history of Chicago is the history of the Middle West. And the history of the Middle West is, to a larger extent than the school textbooks have ever permitted us to discover, the history of the nation.

FLOYD DELL, *author, essayist,*
and editor of the influential
The Friday Review, *May 10, 1912*

Henry James would have been vastly improved as a novelist by a few whiffs from the Chicago stockyards.

H. L. MENCKEN,
The Smart Set, *November 1920*

I do not mean to be at all pharisaic about Chicago. It has many beauties including the fine fastidiousness and good taste to assassinate nobody except assassins.

> G. K. CHESTERTON, *humorist, journalist, and novelist, commenting on the state of lawlessness in Chicago, 1922*

There's only one thing for Chicago to do, and that's to move to a better neighborhood.

> HERMAN FETZER, *humorist, 1930*

Get out of your train and drive up Michigan Avenue! I defy you not to respond to the excitement in the air, not to throw your hat to the sky and shout "Beautiful, how beautiful!" How beautiful it is as you whirl northward past the Tribune Tower.

> MARY BORDEN, *novelist, 1930s*

Chicago: another Pompeii in luxury if not in licentiousness.

ELIAS COLBERT,
historian and journalist, 1872

Chicago: a mushroom and a filthy suburb of Warsaw.

ARNOLD BENNETT, *English author*

Chicago: a pompous Milwaukee.

LEONARD LOUIS LEVINSON,
American author

A facade of skyscrapers facing a lake and behind the facade, every type of dubiousness.

E. M. FORSTER,
English novelist and essayist

Chicago presents more splendid attractions and more hideous repulsions close together than any place known to me.

> *Correspondent,*
> London Daily Mail, *c. 1900*

I find the whiskey unexpectedly good.

> WILLIAM BUTLER YEATS, *Irish poet, visiting*
> *Chicago during Prohibition*

Chicago is over-grown. It is oafish. It shows many of the characteristics of the upstart and the bounder. But under its surface there is a genuine earnestness, a real interest in ideas, a sound curiosity about the prodigal and colorful life of the people of the Republic.

> H. L. MENCKEN, *newspaper*
> *columnist and social critic*

Chicago's greatness, her unique qualities, her amazing rise and advance as a city came from an unusual and balanced combination of the best blood of New England and of the South.

ROBERT SHACKLETON,
The Book of Chicago, *1920*

And I came to love Chicago as one only loves chosen—or lost—cities.

MARGARET ANDERSON,
My Thirty Years War, *1930*

Nobody can think of Chicago as actually existing. A person would go mad if he did. It is a grotesque nightmare and easily recognizable as such.

DON MARQUIS, *New York humorist, 1932*

Chicago is the ideal location for dancing on top of a volcano. Eruptive and exciting, a city of superlatives. It exaggerates all the splendor and squalor in America.

ANNE O'HARE McCORMICK,
*author and Pulitzer Prize-
winning correspondent, 1932*

Four years ago I came to a Chicago fighting with its back to the wall. Factories closed, markets silent, banks shaky, ships and trains empty. Today those factories sing the song of industry—markets hum with bustling movement. Banks are secure; ships and trains are running full. Once again it is Chicago as Carl Sandburg saw it. The City of the Big Shoulders. The city that smiles and, with Chicago, a whole nation that had not been cheerful for years is full of cheer once more.

PRESIDENT FRANKLIN D. ROOSEVELT,
October 14, 1936

Chicago has survived and has maintained an incredibly rapid growth in spite of fires, scandals, corruption, and gang warfare. One feels an indomitable spirit there, an instinct for life.

PEARL S. BUCK, *author*

In the past the wise money has never been on what Chicago could not do. Its motto is "I Will."

GEORGE SESSIONS PERRY,
The Saturday Evening Post, *1947*

I give you Chicago. It is not London and Harvard. It is not Paris and buttermilk. It is American in every chitling and sparerib. It is alive from snout to tail.

H. L. MENCKEN

Chicago seems a big city instead of merely a large place.

A. J. LIEBLING, *humorist, first to
designate Chicago the Second City, 1949*

Never in any other city had I felt surrounded by such an impenetrable density.

> SIMONE DE BEAUVOIR,
> America Day by Day, *1953*

Russians have a great deal of respect for Chicago.

> RICHARD M. NIXON, *after the*
> *Kitchen Debate with Soviet premier*
> *Nikita Khrushchev, August 15, 1959*

An exciting city. I'd like to take it back to Ireland with me.

> TERENCE O'NEILL,
> *Irish prime minister, October 5, 1967*

This is magnificent. What wonderful people! We have not been disappointed. Above all we shall remember the warmth and kindness of your people.

> QUEEN ELIZABETH II *to*
> *Mayor Richard J. Daley, July 7, 1959*

When my parents were here in 1959, I believe the then Mayor Daley suggested that the Queen should come back one day and bring the kids. Well, the Queen's not here. She's in Canada. But I've come back as a rather elderly kid. Thank you very much indeed.

PRINCE CHARLES, *October 20, 1977*

From the bottom of my heart, thank you, Chicago.

PRINCESS DIANA *to luncheon guests at the Drake Hotel, 1996*

No other city in mainland U.S.A. can offer a spectacle like the Loop, where dozens of major buildings lie within the compass of an afternoon stroll.

REYNER BANHAM, *British architectural critic, 1964*

New York is one of the capitols of the world and Los Angeles is a constellation of plastic, San Francisco is a lady, Boston has become urban renewal. Philadelphia and Baltimore and Washington wink like dull diamonds in the smog of Eastern Megalopolis, and New Orleans is unremarkable past the French Quarter. Detroit is a one-trade town, Pittsburgh has lost its golden triangle, St. Louis has become the golden arch of the corporation, and nights in Kansas City close early. The oil-depletion allowance makes Houston and Dallas naught but checkerboards for this sort of game. But Chicago is a great American city. Perhaps it is the last of the great American cities.

NORMAN MAILER, *author,*
Miami and the Siege of Chicago, *1968*

Chicago is basically our loveliest city. It has a tradition of architecture going from Louis Sullivan, Frank Lloyd Wright, and so on. You can see frightful things in Chicago, but there is still modern architecture that can blow the mind with the imagination of its beauty.

CLIVE BARNES, Chicago Daily News, *1974*

When we were in space, we saw Chicago city. It is a very big city [that] has many avenues, has many streets, and a lot of big buildings. But Chicago on the ground is much better than from space.

MAJOR GENERAL ALEXEI A. LEONOV,
Soviet cosmonaut, 1975

A town with a Queen Anne front and a Mary Ann back.

PAUL H. DOUGLAS, New York Times, *1977*

I feel it is the American city, a blend of giant industrialism and the rest of America. New York is a polyglot and to me the connecting link to Europe, whereas I regard Chicago as the heart of America, urban, and that strange blend that Sandburg did such a great job of describing.

ED ASNER, *actor, 1977*

The lake is the fundamental fact of Chicago spiritually as well as geographically. Here the restless, teeming city; the seeming unstoppable city, comes to a stop both abrupt and absolute. There's something almost religious about it.

> HARVEY ARDEN,
> National Geographic, *1978*

It was as if that strongly Irish-Catholic town was destined to produce sexually obsessed native sons, most of whom would eventually exile themselves into more liberal surroundings. Chicago was America's Dublin.

> GAY TALESE, Thy Neighbor's Wife, *1980*

Hell has been described as a pocket edition of Chicago.

> ASHLEY MONTAGU,
> The American Way of Life, *1967*

Chicago has a strange metaphysical elegance of death about it.

CLAES OLDENBURG, *architect*

Chicago stands with all the highs and lows that any human being is capable of. That is the genius of Chicago.

YEHUDI MENUHIN, *violinist, 1976*

Chicago is not only a real city . . . and one of the world's great cities, but at the same time it's a city that's knowable, manageable, and workable. You can figure it out. It has a sense of cohesiveness . . . not like Los Angeles, which is a suburb in search of its soul.

LUCY SALENGER, *Chicago Office
of Film and Entertainment, 1981*

I see Chicago half-emptied by decline, its stately buildings hung with laundry, and children shaking their plastic cups at the intersection. This "Second City" is irrevocably second at best.

JAN MORRIS, *Welsh travel writer, 1988*

There's a freshness, a vitality about the city. It hasn't been corroded with ultra-sophistication and with its citizens' esteeming of their own quality. Yet at the same time it's a magnificent city—the architecture, the music. It's enough to make your mouth drop open.

GERALD ARPINO, *cofounder of the Joffrey Ballet, 1995*

It's one of those cities we feel we know a lot about because it has such a prominent place in the imaginative life of the twentieth century, whether because of Al Capone, Mayor Daley, or Michael Jordan.

SALMAN RUSHDIE, *author of* The Satanic Verses, *out of hiding and in Chicago, January 1996*

There are some cities that are resolutely turned toward the future. Chicago is one of them. Its very size, the beauty of its bold, modern architecture—these are the signs of a powerful, dynamic metropolis full of life and activity.

JACQUES CHIRAC,
president of France, February 1996

Chicago is the glory and damnation of America all rolled up into one. Not to know Chicago is not to know America.

NEAL R. PEIRCE *and* JOHN KEEFE,
The Great Lakes of America, *1980*

Eventually I think that Chicago will be the most beautiful great city left in the world.

FRANK LLOYD WRIGHT, *architect, 1939*

More than a hundred years ago, Mark Twain wrote about your city . . . and what he said then has lost nothing in the passage of time. "That astounding Chicago," wrote Twain. "A city where they are always rubbing the lamp . . . and fetching up the genie . . . and contriving and achieving new possibilities." That would certainly explain Dennis Rodman.

> MICHAEL D. EISNER, *chairman and CEO of the Walt Disney Company, lunchtime address to the Executives Club of Chicago, April 19, 1996*

2

**Empire of
the Prairie**

The winters were long, no railroads, no telegraphs, no canal, and all we had to rely on for news were our weekly newspapers. We had no libraries, no lectures, no theaters, and no other places of amusement. You ask what society lived upon in those days? I answer, upon faith. But faith without works is dead. Our faith consisted principally in the future of Chicago.

JOHN WENTWORTH, *newspaper publisher and mayor of Chicago, 1857, 1860–61*

[T]he love I bear for the city of my birth is inspired not by a material greatness in the achievement of which that railway has no doubt been a factor, but by a spirituality of whose very existence the world at large is still ignorant—seething Chicago, to those who knew her least, being but a soulless place where cattle are handled so swiftly that life itself becomes a raw material.

HOBART C. CHATFIELD-TAYLOR,
socialite, author, patron of the arts,
Cities of Many Men, *1925*

Through the wages I dispense and the provisions I supply, I give more people food than any other man alive.

> PHILIP DANFORTH ARMOUR, *meatpacker,*
> *founder of Armour Institute*

The pigs are kept in large pens under the very roof of the house, driven into a small pen, caught by a pair of tentacles by a hind leg, lifted up and cut in the throat, moved off, cleaned, and suspended. It is curious to see a thousand corpses of hogs suspended in immense rows. In the winter they kill about 1,000 hogs daily. From the bowels of the hogs they boil 75 to 100 barrels of oxen tallow daily. In their smoking houses they each smoke 33,000 hams at once. They cure the hams first in a pickle of sugar, salt peter, and salt. Afterwards they sew them up in a canvass and lager them.

> HEINRICH SCHLIEMANN, *archaeologist,*
> *visited the Chicago Stockyards*
> *in November 1867*

A cow gets lowin' softly into Armour's and comes out glue, gelatine, fertylyzer, celooid, jooolry, sofy cushions, hair restorer, washin' sody, soap, lithrachoor, and bed springs so quick that while she's still cow, for'ard she may be anything fr'm buttons to pannyma hats.

> FINLEY PETER DUNNE (MR. DOOLEY),
> *journalist and humorist, on*
> *what happens to Mr. Armour's pigs*

It is the code of honor among wolves that no high-minded lamb will squeal.

> HENRY DEMAREST LLOYD, *social reformer,*
> *commenting on P. D. Armour in the pages*
> *of the* North American Review, *1883*

I aimed at the public's heart, and by accident I hit it in the stomach.

> UPTON SINCLAIR, *author of the novel*
> The Jungle, *commenting on his*
> *description of the unsanitary*
> *conditions in Packingtown, 1906*

Eyewitnesses to Chicago History

Pioneer Voices

The origin of the name Chicago is a subject of discussion, some of the Indians deriving it from the fighter polecat; others from the wild onion with which the woods formerly abounded; but all agree that the place received its name from an old chief who was drowned in the stream in former times.

JULIETTE KINZIE, *wife of trader*
John Kinzie and author of Wau-Bun:
The Early Days in the Northwest, *1857*

I arrived in Chicago in the year 1826, from Detroit; came with my family by team; no road, only Indian trail. I had to hire an Indian to show me the road to Chicago. I camped outdoors and bought a log house from Jim [sic] Kinzie. There was no town laid out; didn't expect a town.

MARK BEAUBIEN *built the city's first*
hotel—the Sauganash.

Eyewitnesses to Chicago History

Pioneer Voices Continued

The village presented a most motley scene. The fort [Fort Dearborn] contained within its palisades by far the most enlightened residents; in the little knot of officers . . . next to the officers the residents, a doctor or two, two or three lawyers, a land agent, five or six hotel keepers and merchants. Birds of passage, horse drivers, and horse stealers, rogues of every description, white, black, brown, and red. Half-breeds, quarter-breeds, and men of no breed at all; dealers in pigs, poultry, and potatoes . . . creditors, sharpers of every degree, peddlers, grog sellers. The little village was in an uproar from morning until night and from night until morning when the housed population of Chicago strove to obtain repose in the crowded plank edifices of the village. The Indians howled, sang, wept, yelled, and whooped in their encampments. With all this the whites seemed to be more pagan than the red men.

CHARLES J. LATROBE, *English writer, 1833*

Eyewitnesses to Chicago History

Pioneer Voices Continued

The troops behaved most gallantly. They were but a handful. In the meantime, a horrible scene was enacted. One young savage, climbing into the baggage wagon containing the children of the white families, tomahawked nearly all of them.

MARGARET HELM, *survivor of the Fort Dearborn massacre, August 15, 1812*

When whites are killed, it is a massacre. When Indians are killed, it is a fight. So it has ever been, and so it always will be until the last of my color has taken the journey beyond the grave upon which I myself must soon set out.

SIMON POKOGON, *son of Leopold Pokogon, chief of the Potawatomi tribe that attacked Fort Dearborn in 1812. Leopold Pokogon sold the land that became the city of Chicago for three cents an acre.*

Eyewitnesses to Chicago History

Pioneer Voices Continued

You have undoubtedly heard various tales about me. I told you all that I would not be a political Indian any more than what would be of benefit to my red brethren—that is, to take them over the Mississippi in order to draw them from this scene of destruction.

BILLY CALDWELL, *Native-American-Anglo fur trader and merchant, c. 1815*

Oh, Sodom was some and Gomorrah was great—
And in Venice each man's an Iago
But nothing out there can ever compare with the sweet state of things in Chicago.

"Chicago," popular song, 1868

Eyewitnesses to Chicago History

The Great Chicago Fire, October 8, 1871

This is my last public address that will be delivered within these walls! A terrible calamity is impending over the City of Chicago! More I cannot say! More I dare not utter!

> GEORGE FRANCIS TRAIN, *New York author and lecturer, October 7, 1871*

It was the completeness of the wreck, the total desolation which met the eye at every hand; the utter blankness of what had a few hours before been so full of life, of associations, of aspirations, of all things which kept the mind of a Chicagoan so constantly crowded and his nerves and muscles so completely driven.

> ELIAS COLBERT *and* EVERETT CHAMBERLAIN, *chroniclers, November 1871*

Eyewitnesses to Chicago History

The Great Chicago Fire, October 8, 1871 Continued

My poor cow! My poor cow! She is gone, and I have nothing left in the world!

CATHERINE O'LEARY,
342 DeKoven Street, October 11, 1871

The contemptible cow barn on DeKoven Street whose owner is nameless and whose existence was yesterday as utterly unknown as the individuality of any one of the vermin which haunt our streets is today as famous as the Vesuvius whose rage so inundated and buried two great cities that nearly 18 centuries have been required to discover their sepulchre.

Chicago Times, *October 11, 1871*

Eyewitnesses to Chicago History

The Great Chicago Fire, October 8, 1871 Continued

Let us all cheer up and save what is yet left, and we shall come out alright. The Christian world is coming to our relief. The worst is already over. In a few days more all the dangers will be past and we can resume the battle of life with Christian faith and Western grit. Let us all cheer up!

WILLIAM BROSS, Chicago Tribune
editor, October 11, 1871

We have lost money, but we have saved life, health, vigor, and industry. Let the watchword henceforth be, Chicago shall rise again!

JOSEPH MEDILL, Chicago Tribune
publisher, October 11, 1871

Eyewitnesses to Chicago History

The Great Chicago Fire, October 8, 1871 Continued

All gone but wife, children, and energy

> WILLIAM DALE KERFOOT, *Chicago*
> *real estate agent, October 9, 1871*

The Chicago Fire should occur many times. Each successive time the buildings rising smarter, less expensive, more economic, more beautiful . . . America needs to be gone all over again.

> VACHEL LINDSAY, *poet*

There was no color in the street and no beauty—only a maze of wire ropes overhead and dirty flagging stone under foot. Having seen it, I urgently desire never to see it again. It is inhabited by savages.

> RUDYARD KIPLING,
> *visiting postfire Chicago in the 1880s*

Go to Chicago now young men! Hurry there! Old men! Send your sons! You will never again have such a chance to make money!

> WILLIAM "DEACON" BROSS, *editor and*
> *civic booster, reminding New Yorkers*
> *of the opportunity to be found in*
> *postfire Chicago, 1871*

Eyewitnesses to Chicago History

The World's Columbian Exposition

Even more important than the discovery of Columbus which we are gathered together to celebrate is the fact the general government has discovered women.

> BERTHA HONORE PALMER, *socialite,*
> *philanthropist, and chair of the*
> *Lady Board of Managers of the*
> *Chicago World's Fair, dedicating*
> *The Women's Building, May 1, 1893*

Eyewitnesses to Chicago History

The World's Columbian Exposition Continued

Don't pay any attention to the nonsensical claims of that Windy City. Its people couldn't build a world's fair if they won it!

> CHARLES A. DANA, *on Chicago's prospects for securing the proposed 1892 World's Fair, 1890*

Chicago will be the main exhibit of the Columbian Exposition of 1893. No matter what the aggregation of wonders there, the city itself will make the most surprising presentation. Those who go to study the world's progress will find no other result of human force so wonderful, extravagant or peculiar.

> JULIAN RALPH, Harper's Monthly, *1892*

Eyewitnesses to Chicago History

The World's Columbian Exposition Continued

I would crawl back on my venerable legs rather than not see again the only work my age has produced truly worthy of it.

> HENRY ADAMS, *on the World's Columbian Exposition, c. 1893*

Hell, I would exactly as soon take a season ticket to a circus!

> CHARLES FRANCIS ADAMS, *his brother, in response, c. 1893*

The damage wrought by the world's fair will last a half-century.

> LOUIS SULLIVAN, *architect, referring to the fair's largely neoclassical architectural style*

If a stranger's first impression of Chicago is that of the bar-
barous grid-ironed streets, his second is that of the multitude
of mutilated people whom he meets on crutches. Excepting
immediately after a great war, I have never seen so many
mutilated fragments of humanity as one finds in Chicago . . .
and nothing can be done.

> WILLIAM T. STEAD, *commenting on
> Chicago's industrial doldrums in the
> post–World Columbian depression*

It is the most perfect presentation of nineteenth-century indi-
vidualistic industrialism I have ever seen. Chicago is one
hoarse cry for discipline.

> H. G. WELLS

You shall not press upon labor this crown of thorns; you shall
not crucify mankind upon a cross of gold!

> WILLIAM JENNINGS BRYAN, *hours before
> being nominated as the presidential nom-
> inee at the Democratic National Conven-
> tion, Chicago Coliseum, July 9, 1896*

Very pretty, epigramatic, catchy, but to a great extent meaningless . . . but it suited a majority of the convention to a dot. Bryan left the platform and the convention went wild. Seldom has such a demonstration been seen in any public gathering. . . . All the circumstances considered, the scene might be compared in parallel to some extent with the famous hour when the French General Assembly voted the death sentence of Louis XVI. . . .

Chicago Inter-Ocean, *July 10, 1896*

I have been thinking over Bryan's speech. What did he say anyhow?

JOHN PETER ALTGELD *to delegate*
Clarence Darrow, moments after
Bryan concluded his famous speech

I always hunted for customers. If I learned of a man 200 miles away buried in a clearing in a forest who might buy, I got the name of my establishment to him and invited him in.

POTTER PALMER, *merchant prince,*
hotelier, dictator of social customs

It matters not what a man's income is. Reckless extravagance and waste will sooner or later bring him to ruin.

MARSHALL FIELD I, *merchant prince*

When dining at his home on Prairie Avenue you were never forced to listen to long-winded tales of early struggles and subsequent successes, nor were you one-armed by any manifestation of his riches. Furthermore, your fellow guests were not bejewelled females in sheeny gowns or bumptious males who in the smoking room inserted their thumbs in the arm holes of satin waistcoats whilst flicking with pudgy fingers the ashes from the ends of long cigars. On the contrary, your host was a silent man of quiet tastes who took delight in the intimacy of a few seemly friends to whom he extended his hospitality but never his confidence; for if ever a man kept his counsel, it was this merchant prince.

HOBART C. CHATFIELD-TAYLOR,
commenting on the hospitality
of Marshall Field I, 1925

Most men talk too much. Most of my success has been due to keeping my mouth shut.

PHILIP DANFORTH ARMOUR

Chicago is the finest city in the world for the moderate, natural, average man of affairs in which to live. The New Yorker who says Chicago is a city of no luxuries is probably one of that constantly growing number who are insatiable in their greed for the softer things in life.

GUSTAVUS FRANKLIN SWIFT, *meatpacker
and founder of Swift and Company*

I want nothing now but heaven. All right. All peace. Work . . . work . . . work.

CYRUS HALL MCCORMICK,
last words of the "Reaper King"

Eyewitness to Chicago History

The Capsizing of the *Eastland* in the Chicago River, July 24, 1915

I had planned to travel to Michigan City on the *Eastland*, one of those big lake excursion boats so popular in those days. I had my ticket, and my name was on the list of the Western Electric employees on the *Eastland* manifest. The next evening two of my fraternity brothers from Illinois, Walter Straus and Elmer Stumpf, came to our house to pay their condolences. I'll never forget the shocked look on their face when I answered the door.

> GEORGE HALAS *on changing his plans to board the* Eastland; *he founded the Chicago Bears five years later*

I have learned that the secret of success is to be all things to all men; to be friendly with all and intimate with none.

JOHN WENTWORTH

It is *facile princeps* ["hands down"], the city of indifference. Nobody cares about anything. Its nominal motto is "I Will!" Its actual shibboleth "I won't," with the subscription, "Not how good but how cheap is the deed." Poverty of heart, mind, and sympathy are here conjoined. And they glory in the conjunction.

LOUIS HENRI SULLIVAN, *architect*

Had I known in 1890 how long it would take me to preserve a park for the people against their will, I doubt if I would have undertaken it.

AARON MONTGOMERY WARD, *founder of Montgomery Ward and Company and the person most responsible for Grant Park*

My experience is that the greatest aid to efficiency of labor is a long line of men waiting at the gate.

SAMUEL INSULL, *utilities magnate, who was $14 million in debt at the time of his death*

This town of ours labors under one peculiar disadvantage; it is the only great city in the world to which all its citizens have come for the avowed object of making money. There you have its genesis, its end, its object; and there are but a few of us who are not attending to that object very strictly.

HENRY BLAKE FULLER, *pre–Chicago Renaissance author,* With the Procession, *1895*

I have worked . . . I have schemed and dreamed to make us the greatest architects in the world. I have made him see it and kept him at it. And now he dies. Damn! Damn! Damn!

DANIEL BURNHAM, *architect, on the death of his partner and friend John Wellborn Root, January 1891*

The most disappointing thing in my life is to be summoned by men so incompetent and shortsighted.

GEORGE PULLMAN, *founder of the Pullman Palace Car Company and the community bearing his name*

Make no little plans for they have no magic to stir men's blood and probably themselves will never be realized. Make big plans. Aim high in hope and work, remembering that a noble logical diagram once recorded will never die but long after we are gone will be a living thing, asserting with growing intensity.

> DANIEL BURNHAM'S
> *vision of the City Beautiful, 1909*

Never before in the history of mankind—unless it was one part of Roman times—have large fortunes and in some instances egregious fortunes so readily arisen.

> FRANKLIN MACVEIGH, *millionaire*
> *grocer, secretary of the treasury under*
> *President William Howard Taft*

There is nothing like being fired to take the conceit out of a man.

> SAMUEL INSULL

Academic learning beyond the essentials of the grammar grades in public school is a waste of time and waste of money for the boy who is to enter the commercial life. Practically these college presidents stand on the same level as the merchant who sells goods which he knows to be shoddy.

RICHARD TELLER CRANE, *manufacturer*
who endowed manual training courses
for boys in the public high schools

Money is power and dominion. It is wine and women and song. It is art and poetry and music. It is idleness or activity. It is warmth in winter and coolness in the summer. It is clothing and food. It is travel and sport. It is horses and automobiles and silks and diamonds. It is books. It is education. It is self-respect and the respect of others. No one possesses everybody. In life, money means everything. Anybody will do anything to get it.

JOSEPH MEDILL PATTERSON, *grandson of*
Chicago Tribune *publisher Joseph Medill*

The secret of success in my business is to buy up old junk, fix it up a little, and unload it on some other fellows.

> CHARLES TYSON YERKES, *traction*
> *magnate who attempted to build*
> *a streetcar monopoly in Chicago*

All life's a gamble. Some win. Some lose. Today I lost, maybe tomorrow I'll win. That's life.

> JOHN WARNE "BET A MILLION" GATES,
> *stock market speculator and founder of*
> *the American Steel and Wire Company*

Ambition, coupled with energy, is the driving force of mankind.

> PHILIP DANFORTH ARMOUR

The secret of all great undertakings is hard work and self-reliance.

> GUSTAVUS FRANKLIN SWIFT

I was never quite satisfied with anything but always looked forward to doing something better.

GEORGE PULLMAN

The man who cheats the other fellow is a thief, but the man who cheats himself is a fool.

PHILIP DANFORTH ARMOUR

Nothing promotes efficiency in a plant better than an extra man for every job, waiting in a long line at the hiring gate.

CYRUS HALL MCCORMICK

Conspicuous consumption of valuable goods is a means of reputability to the gentlemen of leisure.

THORSTEN VEBLEN,
The Theory of the Leisure Class, *1899*

I never could understand the popular belief that because a man makes a lot of money he has a lot of brains. Some very rich men who made their fortunes have been among the stupidest men I have ever met.

JULIUS ROSENWALD, *philanthropist and chairman of the board of Sears, Roebuck, and Company*

3
Money Talks

I've long respected [President Calvin] Coolidge. He knew when not to talk and what he should not say.

> CHARLES R. WALGREEN, *founder of the Walgreen's drugstore chain, 1932*

Anyone who will lie or steal for you will also lie and steal from you.

> LOUIS GOLDBLATT, *president of the Goldblatt department stores, 1976*

Those who don't [call me "A. N."] call me a son-of-a-bitch.

> ABRAM NICHOLAS "A. N." PRITZKER, *founder of the Hyatt hotel chain*

A man whose heart is in his work can get good thoughts at a ball game.

> CHARLES R. WALGREEN, *1932*

The Chicago Playboy

Hugh Hefner on Providing Entertainment for Men

Hugh M. Hefner, Steinmetz High School Student Council president, class of 1944, founded Playboy *magazine on a shoestring budget in his Northwest Side apartment in 1953.*

I'm an indoor guy and an incurable romantic, so I decided to put together a men's magazine devoted to the subjects I was more interested in—the contemporary equivalent of wine, women, and song, though not necessarily in that order.

The best place in the world to me has always been under the covers.

The magazine was from the very beginning a statement of rebellion without question.

The Chicago Playboy

Hugh Hefner on Providing Entertainment for Men Continued

Playboy exploits sex like *Sports Illustrated* exploits sports.

Marriage is the death of hope.

America loves a redeemed sinner.

On his engagement and
marriage to Kimberly Conrad, 1988

Stop and think about yourself: In all the history of the world there was never anyone else like you, and in all the infinity of time to come there will never be another you.

W. CLEMENT STONE, *founder of the*
Chicago-based Combined Insurance
Company of America (now AON), 1962

The confidence of the American people in the values, the fairness, and the honesty of Sears, Roebuck is the most precious asset this company has. Our motto of satisfaction guaranteed or your money back is a real slogan to be faithfully and promptly executed.

GENERAL ROBERT E. WOOD, *president of Sears, Roebuck, and Company*

I looked beyond the immediate audience and said to blacks, to Hispanics, to Asians, to whites—to dreamers everywhere—that long shots do come in and that the hard work, dedication, perseverance will overcome almost any prejudice and open almost any door. That was my faith then, and it's my faith now. I believe that the greater the handicap, the greater the triumph.

JOHN H. JOHNSON *founded a multimillion-dollar cosmetics and publishing empire in Chicago on $500 he borrowed from his mother*

My philosophy is that too much of the philosophy of business isn't much good.

CHARLES R. WALGREEN, *1932*

Do not fear mistakes. Wisdom is often born of such mistakes. You will know failure. Determine how to acquire the confidence required to overcome it. Reach out.

PAUL GALVIN *founded the Galvin Manufacturing Company in Chicago in 1928 which later became Motorola, a worldwide leader in electronics*

When you reach for the stars you may not quite get one, but you won't come up with a handful of mud either.

LEO BURNETT, *who founded his Chicago advertising agency in 1935*

We must never seek to maintain views of our own on any public question except broadcasting itself. Moreover, we must never try to further either side of any debatable question regardless of our own private and personal sympathies.

> WILLIAM S. PALEY, *president of the*
> *Columbia Broadcasting System (CBS)*
> *and a product of the Maxwell Street*
> *ghetto, in an address to a radio broad-*
> *casters' convention, January 29, 1937*

I have learned that it is far easier to write a speech about good advertising than it is to write a good ad.

> LEO BURNETT, *1961*

JOURNALISM
PUBLISHING.
Advertising is the only business where the inventory goes down in the elevators at night.

> FAIRFAX CONE, *advertising*
> *executive, founded the firm*
> *of Foot, Cone, and Belding*

My father used to speak of men you'd have to stand on tip-toes to talk to. Where are those men today?

> STUART BRENT (NÉ STUART BRODSKY),
> *book merchant, iconoclast, and*
> *host of the 1950s television show "Books*
> *& Brent,"* The Seven Stairs, *1962*

I thought my way out of poverty.

> JOHN JOHNSON, *1989*

Awaken the sleeping giant within you! How? Think. Think with a positive mental attitude.

> W. CLEMENT STONE, Success
> through a Positive Mental Attitude

No one is interested in your self-praise or newspaper publicity other than for gossip purposes.

> LOUIS GOLDBLATT, *1976*

The successful retailer must be passionate about customers.

> BERNARD BRENNAN, *CEO of Montgomery Ward and Company, 1996. Restructuring of Ward's and rival Sears, Roebuck by his brother Ed Brennan during the 1980s led to the dismissal of thousands of long-time store employees—equally passionate about their jobs.*

One of the weaknesses of the average young man of today is that he doesn't know what he wants to do and what he is suited for. It is extremely important for one to know rather early what he is capable of doing. Every man cannot be a bank president or a certified public accountant or an actor or a writer or a doctor. He should early determine what he is suited for temperamentally, what he wants to do above all else, and make that his objective.

ARTHUR ANDERSEN, *1933*

There are a lot of reasons why a fellow comes to work every day. I don't do it for the money. As far as money is concerned, whether I'm doing this or a regular job, I'll earn all I need. And it isn't for the power. What is power? What do you really do with it in twentieth-century America?

> ROBERT PRITZKER, *chairman of*
> *the Cerro-Marmon Group, 1977*

It is much easier to stereotype the opposition—and let thinking and efforts to understand end there—than it is to search for a more complex truth.

> MIKE MCCASKEY,
> *Chicago Bears owner, 1979*

My working day begins when I start to lather my face.

> CHARLES R. WALGREEN, *1932*

I kept getting beat out of deals by other agents. They had cars. But I had to walk. They'd hear of a lead that I found, then they'd beat me to it. I worked harder, saw more people than anyone else. That's what you do—see more people than your competition. Generate the volume.

> ARTHUR RUBLOFF *arrived in Chicago in 1919, opening his real estate firm in 1930 with $730. Arthur Rubloff and Company became the largest Midwestern real estate agent and was the driving force behind the concept of Michigan Avenue's Magnificent Mile.*

I used to have a big house in Chicago. But when I'd go on trips, the yard man would let the grass grow, and the servants would drink up my scotch. We do better living in a hotel.

> *Billionaire* JOHN D. MACARTHUR, *founder of Banker's Life and Casualty, on why he left Chicago for Palm Beach, Florida, 1977. The John D. and Catherine T. MacArthur Foundation was established in 1978 to support the humanities and performing arts.*

The yoke has been lifted. I now have a tremendous amount of free time. I used to have five houses to take care of and now I have the one apartment. There is a liberating feeling in that.

> MICHAEL BUTLER, *polo player,*
> *socialite, ex-hippie, and deal maker,*
> *on his life after bankruptcy*

I learned it all on Maxwell Street. It's the greatest university in the world to teach a guy life and values and struggle and accomplishment and success and disappointment . . . I am the world's greatest sporting goods merchant, and I learned it all on Maxwell Street.

> MORRIE MAGES, Maxwell Street:
> Survival in a Bazaar, *1970*

I don't think about death. I don't like to think about unpleasant things. I want to keep busy and go out of life quietly.

> ARTHUR RUBLOFF

Maxwell Street was never on the tour bus list of places to see. It has squatted for a half-century in the shadows of the rising buildings of the Loop like a bag lady asleep in the doorway of a grand hotel. For about a dozen years, the city has slowly been killing the old market to make way for new neighborhoods, for a university, for new buildings on newly valuable land. The wrecker balls have devastated blocks and blocks in the district roughly bound by Roosevelt Road, 15th Street, Union, and Racine. The remaining buildings in this ghost of a neighborhood are old and broken, and everyone knows that Maxwell Street will be a memory before middle-aged men are dead. But it is a stubborn place, and it tries to stay alive. And on Sundays, summer and winter, in the streets and in the rubble-strewn lots, the peddlers come and claim their spaces before dawn and set up tables and start the fire barrels going and wait for the throng. On Sundays, the ghost haunts the city again.

BILL GRANGER, *newspaper columnist,* Chicago Pieces, *1983*

Never demote a man; instead, dismiss him.

LOUIS GOLDBLATT, *1976*

If you ever find yourself putting major emphasis on counting the money, before long there won't be as much money to count.

LEO BURNETT, *1961*

I am a product of every other black woman before me who has done or said anything worthwhile. Recognizing that I am a part of that history is what allows me to soar. I was raised to believe that excellence is the best deterrent to racism or sexism. And that's how I operate my life.

OPRAH WINFREY, I Dream a World

High Society

New York society may have come over on the *Mayflower*, but Chicago society came over on the Rock Island line.

BOB GREENE, *columnist,*
Johnny Deadline Reporter

One hears so much about the new woman that one is in danger of being bored by her unless she arrives quickly.

> BERTHA HONORE PALMER, *queen of*
> *Chicago society during the Gilded Age*

■ ■ ■

Going to the slammer is no guarantee you'll be dropped from the social register, but dating a carpenter could be.

. . . never get too tan and keep the makeup and body jewelry to a tasteful minimum. Tennis is a better sport than bowling. Bridge and backgammon take precedence over poker and Parchesi, and let *Women's Wear Daily* call you.

> ABRA PRENTICE WILKIN,
> *socialite, advice to social climbers*

■ ■ ■

Yes, we have obligations—we have seen success as a family, and so you try to do your part and give something back, but that's as far as any of us want to go. I'm not a lady who lunches.

> CINDY PRITZKER, *president of the Board of*
> *Directors of the Chicago Public Library*
> *and wife of Jay Pritzker, whose various*
> *family holdings are worth $5 billion*

Cindy, don't talk that way. I'm a tycoon.

> JAY PRITZKER, *when asked to*
> *take out the garbage by his wife*

As everyone knows, the only function served by the society crowd in Chicago is to act as a signal of what has gone out of fashion.

> BOB GREENE, *columnist,*
> Johnny Deadline Reporter

■ ■ ■

Once I called home and said, "Mother, everybody's great-great-grandmother came over on the *Mayflower*." And mother said: "Now dear, you tell them that your ancestors waited until there was better transportation."

It is the little revenges that are the most satisfying.

> SUGAR RAUTBORD (NÉ: DONNA LOU
> KAPLAN), *social arbiter, author
> of* Girls in High Places

■ ■ ■

It was my father's chief desire that I should do something for humanity.

> GEORGE PULLMAN, *sleeping car king*

The way I see it, it does me no good to give money after you're gone—you can't see any results.

> ARTHUR RUBLOFF

4

Acid Ink
and Poison Pens

Chicago has a school of thought! A school of thought which, it is safe to predict, will figure in literature as the school of Chicago for twenty-five years to come.

WILLIAM JAMES, *1904*

During its quick and vivid years—there were hardly nine (1913–22)—Chicago found itself mysteriously a bride of the arts. Not gangster guns, but literary credos barked.

BEN HECHT, *playwright,*
journalist, A Child of the Century, *1954*

It is universally conceded that Chicago is rapidly achieving worldwide reputation as the great literary center in the United States.

EUGENE FIELD, *journalist and*
author of the "Sharps and Flats"
column in the Chicago Daily News

I have seen in Chicago examples of art by local artists fit to grace a grand salon in Paris.

OSCAR WILDE, *1882*

He comes! The simpering Oscar comes!
The West awaits with wonder
As bullfrogs list to beating drums
Or hearken to the thunder

The women pause with bated breath
With wild and wistful faces
And silent as the halls of death
Seem all our public places

He comes with words sublimely dull
In a garb superbly silly
To tell us of the beautiful
The sunflower and the lily

VICTOR LAWSON *and* MELVILLE STONE, *publishers of the* Chicago Daily News, *and their mocking tribute to the foppish Oscar Wilde during his 1882 Chicago visit*

Find a writer who has something American to say and nine times out of ten you will find he has some connection with the gargantuan abattoir by Lake Michigan—he was bred there—or got his start there or passed through there when he was young and tender.

> H. L. MENCKEN,
> The American Mercury, *1933*

I write, and why? I write because I must. I have to say, and none with whom to speak.

> HENRY BLAKE FULLER, *Victorian-era*
> *realist and author of* The Cliff-Dwellers
> *and* With the Procession

For a city where, I am credibly informed, you couldn't throw an egg in 1925 without braining a great poet, Chicago is hard up for writers.

> A. J. LIEBLING,
> Chicago: The Second City, *1952*

Every rhinestone that wants to pass for a diamond instinctively moves to Broadway.

> GEORGE ADE, *columnist, social
> critic, and author,* Fables in Slang

When I visit any other great city of the world, I am a guest. When I am in Chicago, I am at home.

> SHERWOOD ANDERSON,
> *novelist,* Memoirs, *1942*

. . . Sherwood Anderson is a man of practically no ideas—but he is one of the very best and finest writers in the English language today. God, he can write.

> F. SCOTT FITZGERALD, *1925*

It is given to some cities, as to some lands, to suggest romance, and to me Chicago did that hourly. It sang, I thought, and in spite of what I deemed my various troubles, I was singing with it.

> THEODORE DREISER, *novelist,*
> A Book about Myself, *1922*

I read Dreiser's *Jennie Gerhardt* and *Sister Carrie,* and they revived in me a vivid sense of my mother's suffering. I was overwhelmed. I grew silent, wondering about the life around me. I bought a ream of paper and tried to write.

> RICHARD WRIGHT, *author of* Native Son

Chicago: enchanted ground to me from the moment Lake Michigan entered the train windows. I would make my beautiful life here. A city without a lake wouldn't have done.

> MARGARET ANDERSON,
> *editor,* My Thirty Years War, *1930*

Here of all her cities, throbbed the true life—the true power and spirit of America. Arrogant in the new found knowledge of its giant strength, prodigal of its wealth, infinite in its desires.

FRANK NORRIS, The Pit, *1903*

When I was young, I longed to write a great novel that should win me fame. Now that I am getting old, my first book is written to amuse children. For, aside from my evident inability to do anything great, I have learned to regard fame as a will-o'-the-wisp, which when caught, is not worth the possession. But to please a child is a sweet and lovely thing that warms one's heart and brings its own reward. I hope my book will succeed in that way—that the children will like it.

LYMAN FRANK BAUM, *in a letter to his sister Mary Louise Baum Brewster. L. Frank Baum wrote* The Wonderful Wizard of Oz *in Chicago in 1900.*

All the afternoon and evening we wandered about the streets (being very careful not to go too far from our hotel), counting the stories of the tall buildings, absorbing the drama of the pavement. Everything interested us. The business section so sordid to others was grandly terrifying to us. The self-absorption of the men. The calm glances of the women humbled our simple souls. Nothing was commonplace, no thing was ugly to us.

HAMLIN GARLAND,
Son of the Middle Border, *1917*

We left the Fine Arts Building with fresh copies of *The Little Review* under our arms—we who were lucky enough to be in it—and felt big in the street—anointed but unknown, which was the *shekinah* [the divine presence] of the true artist.

BEN HECHT, A Child of the Century, *1954*

Here's the difference between us and Dante. He wrote a lot about hell and never saw the place. We're writing about Chicago after looking the town over.

> CARL SANDBURG, *poet and*
> *newspaper reporter who came*
> *to Chicago in 1913. In 1951 he*
> *won the Pulitzer Prize for poetry.*

I had been happy in Chicago; never would it seem to me a gray and ugly city. I loved the lake, Michigan Boulevard with its open vista and its gleaming lights; the parks, even the preposterous Loop district with its sudden architectural leap into the sky; I had seen beauty there, enough to fill my heart; there had been days and nights of talk and laughter; the years had passed in a golden glow of friendship; and it was a city haunted everywhere by the memories of love, its pain and glory.

> FLOYD DELL, *on leaving Chicago in 1913*

Chicago has very little respect for the seventeenth century because there is nothing in it. The seventeenth century has done nothing for Chicago; she doesn't even know this is the greatest hog market in the world.

EUGENE FIELD

Chicago is not an articulate town, Saul Bellow notwithstanding. Maybe it's because so many of us aren't that far removed from parents and grandparents who knew only bits of the language.

MIKE ROYKO,
columnist, December 21, 1976

People just want to discuss Studs Lonigan. Well, he died. I tell them to wait until they get to heaven, and they can talk to him themselves.

JAMES T. FARRELL, *on coping with the fame of his fictional Chicago hero, Studs Lonigan*

The din of the city entered my consciousness; entered to remain for years to come.

> RICHARD WRIGHT, *on coming
> to Chicago in 1927 at age nineteen*

. . . here was somebody named Nelson Algren writing about Division Street and Milwaukee Avenue, and the dopeheads and boozers and the card hustlers. The kind of broken people Algren liked to describe as responding to the city's brainy slogan of "I Will" with a painful "But what if I can't?"

> MIKE ROYKO, *May 13, 1981*

A thought occurs to me. Had my luck been better, I might have become a first-class pimp or a candidate for public office or even an adviser to presidents.

> STUDS TERKEL, *author, critic, talk
> show host, raconteur,* Talking to
> Myself: A Memoir of My Times, *1977*

Chicago, it seems, has a way of leaving its imprint upon those who live in it.

RICHARD WRIGHT

Loving Chicago is like loving a woman with a broken nose.

NELSON ALGREN

No realistic sane person goes around Chicago without protection.

SAUL BELLOW

Chicago: It's still a frontier town.

NORMAN MARK, *author and television personality,* Mayors, Madams, and Madmen, *1979*

Chicago is an October sort of city even in the Spring.

NELSON ALGREN

Posterity—what you write for after being turned down by publishers.

GEORGE ADE

A good many young writers make the mistake of enclosing a stamped self-addressed envelope big enough for the manuscript to come back in. This is too much of a temptation to the editor.

RING LARDNER, *author and essayist who wrote the "Wake of the News" column in the* Chicago Tribune

. . . if James Jones, who is a fourth-rate writer, . . . is worth three-quarters of a million, then I must be worth Fort Knox.

NELSON ALGREN

You write a book, you invest your imagination in it, and then you hand it over to a bunch of people who have no imagination and no understanding of their own enterprise.

SAUL BELLOW

No one ever wrote anything as well even after one drink as he would have done without it.

RING LARDNER

Art attempts to find in the universe, in matter as well as in the facts of life, what is fundamental, enduring, essential.

SAUL BELLOW, *1976*

Sanity in art—sanity in everything—is indeed a fine goal at which to aim, but the question immediately arises: Whose sanity?

CHAUNCEY MCCORMICK,
Art Institute Board of Trustees

I cannot think of art as a mere adornment of life—a frill on human existence—but life itself.

> LORADO TAFT, *sculptor*

Live fast, die young, and have a good-looking corpse.

> WILLARD MOTLEY,
> Knock on Any Door, *1947*

I have fallen short of almost everything I have undertaken, but what a good time I have had in failing.

> LORADO TAFT

We don't have much use for poetry in Chicago—except in streetcar ads.

> GEORGE HORACE LORIMER,
> The Saturday Evening Post

The people must grant a hearing to the best poets, 'else they will never have better.

HARRIET MONROE, *editor,*
Poetry Magazine

Poetry is the achievement of the synthesis of hyacinths and biscuits.

CARL SANDBURG, *1923*

It used to be a writer's town, and it's always been a fighter's town. For writers and fighters and furtive torpedoes, cat-bandits, baggage thieves, hallway headlockers on the prowl, baby photographers, and stylish coneroos, this is the spot that is always most convenient, being so centrally located for settling ancestral grudges. Whether the power is in a .38, a typewriter ribbon, or a pair of six-ouncers, the place has grown great on bone-deep grudges of writers and fighters and furtive torpedoes.

NELSON ALGREN,
Chicago: City on the Make, *1951*

Whenever the subject of good Chicago writers comes up, I find it really tiresome that people always trot out Algren and Bellow.

> SHARON SLOAN FIFFER, *author and*
> *former editor of* Other Voices, *1995*

Nelson Algren is dead, and Saul Bellow doesn't live here anymore.

> CONNIE GODDARD, *Chicago*
> *literary agent and editor*

I, Stuart Brent, have become an anachronism. I was fading out, coming up empty, day after day after day. I don't have the loyalty of discerning readers who used to come to me for books by Joyce, Proust, Spengler; for the books on psychoanalysis and literature that my bookstore was noted for . . . It's apparent that this marvelous city and its crown jewel, Michigan Avenue, have been reduced to brown popcorn.

> STUART BRENT, *on the closing*
> *of his famous Michigan Avenue*
> *bookstore in January 1996*

I loved Chicago. I could never forget it. I would come back to it. But I must go on. I told everyone good bye including the Fine Arts Building. I went to work through its corridors which always seemed to be filled with flowers—its shops which gave me the emotion of a perpetual Christmas. Last of all I went to a symphony concert. Coming back to the Fine Arts Building, I met Ben Hecht. "After you are gone," he announced, "I'm going to have an electric sign put across this building."

"Where is Athens now?"

MARGARET ANDERSON, *on leaving Chicago, closing* The Little Review, *and moving to New York*

5

Athletes' Feats

In the fantasy of my dreams I have imagined myself as the announcer for a Cubs-White Sox World Series, a series that would last seven games, with the final game going extra innings before being suspended because of darkness at Wrigley Field.

> JACK BRICKHOUSE, *Hall of Fame*
> *broadcaster who covered the Cubs*
> *and Sox for nearly forty-five years*

Jack Brickhouse has seen more bad baseball than any person living or dead.

> STEVE DALEY, *former*
> Chicago Tribune *sports columnist*

I would love to call the wives together some day and tell them what their husbands say about them across the hall. I just tell the truth, and they think it's hell.

> HARRY CARAY, *broadcaster*
> *of the White Sox and the Cubs, 1981*

■ ■ ■

What good was all the fame for Joe Louis or for me? There was no avenue to capitalize. No advertising, no endorsements because the South wouldn't buy us.

First you must have the dream. It all begins with the dream.

> JESSE OWENS, *Olympian and*
> *winner of four gold medals*
> *at the 1936 Berlin Olympics*

■ ■ ■

Nothing on Earth is more depressing than an old baseball writer.

> RING LARDNER *wrote the* Chicago
> Tribune's *"Wake of the News" column,*
> *where he conceived his famous "You*
> *Know Me Al" series of baseball spoofs*

To me baseball is as honorable as any other business. It is the most honest pastime in the world. It has to be, or it could not last a season out. Crookedness and baseball do not mix. It has become immeasurably more popular as the years have gone by. It will be greater yet! This year, 1919, is the greatest season of them all!

White Sox owner CHARLES COMISKEY, *on the eve of the 1919 World Series, just before eight of his star players accepted money for throwing the World Series to the Cincinnati Redlegs*

I have played a crooked game, and I have lost.

ED CICOTTE, *Chicago White Sox pitcher banned in 1921 for conspiring with seven teammates to throw the 1919 World Series*

When I die, I hope to die with number nine on my back.

MINNIE MINOSO, *"Mr. White Sox"*

Say it ain't so, Joe!

> *Anonymous youngster to "Shoeless" Joe*
> *Jackson, outside the Criminal Courts*
> *Building, September 1920, after Jackson's*
> *role in the Black Sox scandal was*
> *exposed. Originally reported by Don M.*
> *Ewing of the Associated Press, the quote*
> *is likely an apocryphal one.*

When I pulled the crimson sweater over my head, my only thought was not to embarrass myself, my teammates, my family, my organization. Everything I did was with pride.

> BOBBY HULL, *the "Golden Jet" of*
> *the Chicago Blackhawks, 1957–72*

Everyman's great moment on the Sox comes when no one is watching.

> JEAN SHEPARD, *humorist and Sox fan*

■ ■ ■

I have always found humor in the incongruous. I have always tried to entertain.

My friends are the fans, not the owners. Dignity isn't my suit of clothes.

BILL VEECK *owned the White Sox*
in 1959–61 and 1976–80

■ ■ ■

I view myself as being in politics. You get elected if you have 50.1 percent of the vote. I'm not in it for approval of 100 percent of the fans. I just try to do a good job. . . . Public opinion doesn't affect my decisions. That doesn't mean I like being ripped because I don't. But I don't let opinions control me.

JERRY REINSDORF, *White Sox owner,*
on handling media criticism, 1993

I'm not Mr. Smooth Talker, as you can see from my reputation in this town. When I've got something to say, I come out and say it. If anything, that's what I can offer to this game. I will be real. I'd rather be myself than talk a bunch of bullshit that doesn't mean anything.

> JACK MCDOWELL, *former White Sox*
> *pitching ace, showed his real self*
> *to Yankee fans when he flipped them*
> *an obscene gesture after stalking*
> *off the mound, July 18, 1995*

These are the saddest of possible words—
Tinker to Evers to Chance
Trio of Bear Cubs and fleeter than birds
Tinker to Evers to Chance
Thoughtlessly pricking our gonfalon bubble
Making a giant hit into a double—
Words that are weighty with nothing but trouble—
Tinker to Evers to Chance

> FRANKLIN P. ADAMS, *verse celebrating the*
> *1906 Chicago Cubs infield, composed*
> *while working for the* Chicago Journal

We believe that baseball is a daytime sport, and we will continue to play it in the sunshine as long as we can.

PHILIP WRIGLEY,
former owner of the Chicago Cubs

I've never played drunk. Hungover, yes. But never drunk!

HACK WILSON, *Chicago Cubs*
outfielder and social drinker, 1930s

The Cubs are not an eighth-place ball club!

LEO DUROCHER, *upon taking over*
as Cub manager after the 1965
season; the Cubs finished tenth in 1966

It's always a beautiful day for baseball. Let's play two!

ERNIE BANKS, *"Mr. Cub" and*
member of the Baseball Hall of Fame

I like my players to be married and in debt. That's the way you motivate them.

ERNIE BANKS, *speaking as a coach, 1976*

I don't have the natural ability that some of those guys do, so I use smarts in the field.

MARK GRACE, *Chicago Cubs
all-star first baseman, 1996*

In Chicago, we may not think the Picasso presiding over the Richard J. Daley Center plaza is art, but we know it's a big Picasso and it's the city's Picasso, and when the Cubs made the play-offs, the sculpture wore a baseball cap just like everything else.

PAT COLANDER, New York Times, *1985*

You go to every game hoping this one will be the turn. Then they screw up, and your hope turns bitter. By the end of the game, you hate every man on the team and Halas, too. It's love going in, hate coming out. But by Wednesday your hopes go up again.

> JOHN FISCHETTI, *Pulitzer Prize-winning*
> *cartoonist for the* Chicago Daily News,
> *on rooting for the Chicago Bears*

■ ■ ■

I had no particular ambitions as a child other than being a baseball player. It wasn't until I was a sophomore at Crane Tech High School that I recognized that I'd never be a genius and that to get anywhere, I would have to work hard. I've been working hard ever since.

> GEORGE HALAS, *1976*

I really feel sorry for the Yankees. They had to replace me with a reconditioned pitcher from Boston named Babe Ruth.

> HALAS *gave up pro baseball in*
> *1920 to found the Chicago Bears*

■ ■ ■

Being famous is bunk . . . I've never felt worse. I'll never marry unless I find someone far more sensible than the flappers who flock around. I'll never be a millionaire. I'm glad I turned pro, but I'll be glad to quit.

> HAROLD "RED" GRANGE, *the*
> *"Galloping Ghost" of the Chicago Bears*

The same fellows who advised me not to play professional football wound't lend me a dollar if I were broke.

> O*n turning pro*

■ ■ ■

What a football player—this man Red Grange. He is a melody and symphony. He is crashing sound. He is brute force.

> *Sportswriter* DAMON RUNYON,
> *on the "Galloping Ghost"*

■ ■ ■

I never had a philosophy other than whip the other guy.

What you do in life by yourself doesn't mean as much as what you accomplish with a group of people.

Man, this is what football is all about—people getting the snot kicked out of them!

> MIKE DITKA, *Chicago Bears tight end,*
> *1961–66, and Bears' coach, 1982–92*

■ ■ ■

It scares me just to have millionaires opening doors for me.

> *All-American halfback* GALE SAYERS,
> *on being escorted to Chicago by*
> *millionaire tycoon Lamar Hunt to*
> *sign his first pro contract with*
> *the Chicago Bears, December 1964*

I am deeply satisfied that Yale has come here. But I have always been guided by duty rather than emotion. My duty and the duty of my team is to beat Yale.

> AMOS ALONZO STAGG, *coach of the*
> *University of Chicago Maroons, on*
> *the eve of the big game against*
> *his alma mater, October 17, 1931*

The pressure goes with the job. It's just when I'm driving home and there are two or three guys following me with cameras, hanging out their windows to see if I'll signal when I make a right turn—then it gets tough.

> WALTER PAYTON, *Chicago Bears*
> *running back who surpassed*
> *Jim Brown's career rushing record in 1984*

I love the game of football, but I sure hate what it does to people who play it.

> JEANNIE MORRIS, *sportscaster and wife*
> *of Johnny Morris of the Chicago Bears*

I'm entitled to my opinion, so I'll go on record as saying board chairman Ed McCaskey's rendition of "Bear Down, Chicago Bears" sounds like a cross between Rudy Vallee and Placido Domingo.

> JACK BRICKHOUSE,
> Thanks for Listening, *1986*

When I started, I'd walk the streets all night after a loss. I couldn't eat or sleep. As the years went by, I came to realize losing is as much a part of coaching as winning. The game is a slice of life. There is good in every experience if you learn from it.

> RAY MEYER *coached the DePaul basketball team from 1942 to 1984, winning 724 and losing 354 games.*

He's more than a great coach—he's a developer of men.

> GEORGE MIKAN, *All-American DePaul Blue Demons forward, on Ray Meyer*

That's alright
That's okay
You'll work for us some day

> ~~Halftime~~ *chant at Dyche Stadium*
> *when the going gets rough for the*
> *Northwestern Wildcats*

We're probably at least five years from competing for the Rose Bowl. I hope I'm wrong. I hope we can do it this year. We're going to do it? Aren't we, president? Aren't we, athletic director? I mean that's why I'm here. So aren't we, guys?

> *Northwestern Wildcat coach*
> GARY BARNETT, *September 1994. The Cats*
> *went to the Rose Bowl the following year*
> *for the first time since 1949.*

I discovered I could be far more effective as a coach when I balanced the masculine and feminine sides of my nature.

> *Chicago Bulls coach*
> *and Zen master* PHIL JACKSON

■ ■ ■

Ten years ago I was just a kid scared to death, leaving high school, wondering if I could play at the next level. Now, ten years later, I'm at the highest level. Ten years down the road no one would ever remember Michael Jordan the challenger.

Michael Jordan, 1991

I'm back.

Coming out of retirement, 1995

■ ■ ■

He's the greatest athlete I've ever seen, maybe the greatest athlete to play any sport. He can do whatever he wants. He's not just a basketball player.

Bulls teammate
Bill Cartwright, on Michael Jordan

Perhaps it was just a reflection of the spiritual malaise of the culture and our desperate yearning for a mystic hero to set us free.

> PHIL JACKSON, *on the media hype*
> *surrounding Michael Jordan's*
> *1995 return to basketball*

This is what I am. I wasn't always like this. It took me a while to find my identity and what I wanted to do and which direction I wanted to go. I don't try to be a big, big role model for kids. But kids look at me as independent and happy and free, and I love what I am doing, and that is more of a role model than anything.

> DENNIS RODMAN,
> *controversial Chicago Bulls forward*

The athletic field is one of the university's laboratories and by no means the least important one.

> WILLIAM RAINEY HARPER, *founding*
> *president of the University of Chicago*

I would rather be a lampost in Chicago than a millionaire in any other city.

> WILLIAM HULBERT, *Chicago business executive who owned the Chicago White Stockings (Cubs) in 1876. He took over as president of the National League a year later*

Football isn't meant to be played for money.

> BOB ZUPPKE *coached Red Grange at the University of Illinois*

6

Crime and
Punishment

Chicago is the greatest law-abiding city in the world.

> MYRA COLBY BRADWELL, *the first*
> *woman admitted to the Illinois Bar*

Chicago ain't no sissy town!

> *First Ward Alderman*
> MICHAEL "HINKY DINK" KENNA

Chicago, a gaudy circus beginning with the two-bit whore in the alley crib.

> THEODORE DREISER

It's not the ladies they like best . . . really. They like cards. They like dice, and horse racing the best. If it wasn't unmanly to admit it, they'd rather most of the time gamble than screw.

> MINNA EVERLEIGH, *co-owner of the*
> *Everleigh Club, Chicago's most luxurious*
> *brothel 1900–11; commenting on her*
> *usual clientele*

The Scales of Justice

When we were kids, my mother used to ask, "Have you done your *mitzvah,* your good deed for the day?" If I hadn't been extending a helping hand, I'd have wound up a punch-drunk fighter instead of a federal judge.

> JUDGE ABRAHAM LINCOLN MAROVITZ,
> *the last federal jurist to be appointed*
> *to the bench without a law degree*

The men who administer the laws are human, with all the failings of humanity. They take their biases, their prejudices with them on to the bench. Upon the whole they try to do the best they can, but the wrongs done in the courts of justice themselves are so great that they cry to heaven.

> JOHN PETER ALTGELD,
> *governor of Illinois, 1893–97*

Laws should be like clothes. They should fit the people they are meant to serve.

CLARENCE DARROW, *1924*

If the exercise of constitutional rights will thwart the effectiveness of a system of law enforcement, then there is something very wrong with that system.

ARTHUR J. GOLDBERG, *former associate justice of the Supreme Court, born in the 800 block of Washburne Avenue near Maxwell Street*

There is no warmth or humanity in the law. It isn't meant to be that way.

JAMES R. THOMPSON, *governor of Illinois, 1976–90, now a partner in the Chicago law firm of Winston and Strawn*

Why is there always a secret singing when a lawyer cashes in?
Why does a hearse horse snicker, hauling a lawyer away?

CARL SANDBURG

If we win the case, no one will remember us. If we lose this
case, no one will forget us.

WILLIAM MARTIN, *author and attorney, to
the prosecution team on the eve of the
Richard Speck trial. Speck murdered
eight student nurses in July 1966.*

One thing we don't have a lot of is role models for women
lawyers. I am a role model. My whole damn life I've been a
role model by just being there.

SUSAN GETZENDANNER, *on her
resignation as a federal judge to join
the law firm of Skadden and Arps, 1990*

■ ■ ■

The second-story man, the safecracker, and the dip are not the only thieves; you'll find a lot in Loop offices.

Reform is here to stay, and Chicago is no place for a gentleman.

> JIM O'LEARY, *son of Catherine O'Leary (of cow and lantern fame) and gambler boss of the Stockyards District, c. 1911*

■ ■ ■

There's a sucker born every minute.

> MICHAEL CASSIUS MCDONALD, *gambling boss of the Gaslight era who owned the Store, a "protected" downtown casino, c. 1875*

We established our government in the deestrict [sic] of Lake Michigan without any flourish of authority or blare of trumpets, and, in fact, without any unique demonstration. One of my outhouses was converted into a temple of justice, and a sign was placed above its door proclaiming its august character. Our deliberations, elections, and other necessary assemblages were held in this building until the police authorities of Chicago regarded it with secret disfavor.

> GEORGE WELLINGTON "CAP" STREETER,
> *squatter, established the "Deestrict*
> *of Michigan" in 1898, near what is now*
> *the posh Streeterville neighborhood*

The World According to Al Capone

You can get much farther with a smile, a kind word, and a gun than you can with a smile and a kind word.

Public service is my motto.

They talk about me not being legitimate. Nobody's on the legit! You know that, and so do they.

You can't blame me for thinking there's worse guys in the world than me.

They blamed everything but the Chicago Fire on me.

When I steal liquor, they call it bootlegging. When my patrons serve it on silver trays on Lake Shore Drive, they call it hospitality.

People who respect nothing dread fear. It is upon fear, therefore, that I have built my organization.

I make my money by supplying a public demand. If I break the law, my customers, who number hundreds of the best people in Chicago, are as guilty as I am. The only difference is that I sell and they buy.

I've given the public what the public wants. I never had to send out high-pressure salesmen. I could never meet the demand.

I have always been opposed to violence. I want peace, and I will live and let live.

Viewpoints of the Opposition

I can whip this bird Capone with my bare fists.

> EDWARD "SPIKE" O'DONNELL, *leader of a South Side bootleg gang, who was shot on September 25, 1925. He survived, but chose a different line of work.*

■ ■ ■

There's $30 million worth of beer sold in Chicago every month, and a million dollars a month is spread among police, politicians, and federal agents to keep it flowing. Nobody in his right mind will turn his back on a share of a million dollars a month.

I don't know anything about any murders. I'm a respectable businessman.

> DION O'BANNION, *boss of the*
> *North Side, was assassinated*
> *by Capone's mob in November 1924.*

■ ■ ■

Only Al Capone kills like that.

> GEORGE "BUGS" MORAN, *boss of*
> *the North Side mob, responding*
> *to questions about the murder*
> *of seven of his men in a Clark*
> *Street garage, February 14, 1929*

You've lost your job
You've lost your dough
Your jewels and handsome houses
But things could be worse, you know
You haven't lost your trousers

> *Comic valentine deposited on the*
> *body of* "MACHINE GUN" JACK MCGURN,
> *mastermind of the Saint Valentine's*
> *Day massacre, moments after he was shot*
> *dead at a Milwaukee Avenue bowling*
> *alley; February 15, 1936*

My father was a Chicago policeman and an honest one. Otherwise he would have had a hell of a lot less trouble getting up the grocery and rent money.

> ROGER TOUHY, *Prohibition-era gangster*
> *framed by Capone for kidnapping and*
> *sent "away" for twenty-six years*

Never trust a woman or an automatic pistol.

> JOHN DILLINGER, *bank robber*
> *who was killed outside the*
> *Biograph Theater in July 1934*

I never cheated honest men, only rascals. They may have been respectable, but they were never any good. They wanted something for nothing. I gave them nothing for something.

> JOSEPH "YELLOW KID" WEIL,
> *legendary con man*

I don't know nothin' about nothin', and I can prove it.

> ED "BUTCH" PANCZKO, *one of four*
> *thieving Panczko brothers who plied*
> *their trade in Chicago for nearly*
> *forty-five years*

Never break into a building more than one story tall in case the cops start shooting, 'cause if the bullets don't kill you, the fall will.

JOSEPH "POPS" PANCZKO, *self-styled thief*

I tell you, if there's a legit cop who hasn't got his hand out, he hasn't caught me yet, so I've never met him.

PAUL "PEANUTS" PANCZKO,
the brains of the outfit

Chicago is as full of crooks as a saw with teeth. But the era when they ruled the city is gone forever.

JOHN GUNTHER, Inside the U.S.A., *1947*

We don't have any more gangsters than any other city. It's just that our gangsters have better press agents.

Chicago tour bus guide, 1962

We don't have well-thought out crimes anymore—no imaginative stick-ups or burglaries for example.

JIM CASEY, Chicago Sun-Times *reporter*

7

Clout City

Politics Chicago Style

clout/*klaut n* pull, influence (political)

Clout is used to circumvent the law, not to enforce it. It is used to bend rules, not follow them.

MIKE ROYKO, *June 7, 1973*

Clout has become a function of skill.

ANTON VALUKAS, *former U.S. attorney general*

Chicago is unique. It is the only completely corrupt city in America.

PROFESSOR CHARLES MERRIAM,
*political economist, reformer, and
unsuccessful mayoral candidate in 1911*

Chicago is not the most corrupt American city. It's the most theatrically corrupt.

STUDS TERKEL, *1978*

It's not true we have a typed-up list of the rate for bribes. We do it all by telephone.

City Hall, anonymous, 1912

It is alright perhaps for a Republican to go heavy on the reform stuff. But in a big city like Chicago with its melting pot character, a Democrat doesn't fit into a fanatical reform picture. A Democrat is supposed to speak for the great masses and not the big fellows . . . Silk-hatting the LaSalle Street crowd is alright if you have been reared in that atmosphere and are one of them. But to give the impression that you've gone over to the silk-hatters after you've been raised under a fedora is fatal in politics in Chicago.

Anonymous West Side alderman,
Sherman House Hotel, April 9, 1925

The Democratic machine is wealthy, strong, and deceptive.

ALDERMAN ROBERT E. MERRIAM,
candidate for mayor, April 1955

We all have jobs that don't interfere with our daily lives.

Anonymous city employee, 1970s

Corruption is not a Democratic problem nor a Republican problem. It is a human problem.

RICHARD J. DALEY,
candidate for mayor, March 31, 1955

There's no loyalty in politics. There's only alliances.

WILLIAM NOLAN, *elected president of
the Fraternal Order of Police, 1993*

Political theoreticians who delve into an analysis of the Democratic machine of Chicago sometimes get misled, I think, by the sheer simplicity of it all.

LEN O'CONNOR, *journalist,
author, and political commentator*

■ ■ ■

Most of them New Yorkers—when they get 100 miles from Broadway, they think they're campin' out. Let me tell you, they ain't the only ones. There are more yaps [hicks] to th' square inch in Chicago than in Oberlin, Ohio. Why, there's lots of people in Chicago who ain't ever been west of the Des Plaines River or south of Grand Crossing.

Rome? Most everybody in Rome has been dead two thousand years. Monte Carlo? Great place! I spent two days there and broke even. I didn't [even] play!

When I see a reformer, I put a hand on my watch.

> FIRST WARD ALDERMAN "BATHHOUSE"
> JOHN COUGHLIN, *on traveling east and west,* Lords of the Levee: The Story of Bathhouse and Hinky Dink, *1943*

■ ■ ■

■ ■ ■

First we counted the voters, then we counted the votes.

> MICHAEL "HINKY DINK" KENNA, *Democratic alderman of the First Ward, 1897–1923*

Why did they build that damned lake next to this city?

> MICHAEL "HINKY DINK" KENNA, *"Bathhouse" John's partner-in-crime*

■ ■ ■

Mr. Mayor, you won because of the public satisfaction with the well-known honesty that has caricatured your every administration!

> "BATHHOUSE" JOHN *to Mayor Carter Harrison after he defeated Graeme Stewart in 1903*

He tells them how to vote, a duty they might otherwise neglect, and sees that they do it properly. And whenever you want to do things in Chicago, you must reckon carefully with him.

> H. G. WELLS, *English author,*
> *commenting on "Hinky Dink" Kenna*

Mike Kenna spoke sparingly. He was a deep thinker and could say a lot in very few words. When he did say anything, it was always to the point, but the "Bath" possessed an uneducated but natural intelligence and an Irish wit that often helped him when debating to stop some of his college-bred opponents on the floor of the City Council.

> CHARLES H. HERMANN, *employee of*
> *Chapin and Gore, a famous Chicago*
> *restaurant,* Recollections of Life and
> Doings in Chicago by an Old Timer, *1945*

In most places in the country, voting is looked upon as a right and a duty. But in Chicago it's a sport. In Chicago not only your vote counts, but all kinds of other votes, kids, dead folks. . . .

> DICK GREGORY, Political Primer, *1972*

I'm wetter than the Atlantic Ocean! When I'm elected, we'll not only reopen places those places those people have closed down, but we'll open ten thousand new ones!

MAYOR WILLIAM HALE THOMPSON'S
campaign pledge to reopen the
taverns shut down by his
predecessor William Dever, 1927

They was trying to beat Bill with the better-element vote. The trouble with Chicago is that there ain't much better element.

WILL ROGERS, *American humorist,*
commenting on William Hale
Thompson's 1927 mayoral victory

To hell with the public! We're at the trough now, and we're going to feed!

FRED "THE POOR SWEDE" LUNDIN, *former*
North Side congressman who served as
Bill Thompson's campaign manager, 1915

Put people under obligation to you. Make them your friends.

> JAKE ARVEY, *Twenty-Fourth Ward*
> *alderman and Democratic Party*
> *boss for nearly three decades*

We want Roosevelt! We want Roosevelt! Illinois wants Roosevelt! Texas wants Roosevelt! New York wants Roosevelt! [Mayor] Kelly wants Roosevelt! Everybody wants Roosevelt!

> THOMAS GARRY, *city superintendent of*
> *sewers, sequestered directly under the*
> *speaker's platform at the Democratic*
> *Convention held at the Chicago Stadium,*
> *July 16, 1940, and booming the Franklin*
> *Roosevelt third-term message across the*
> *hall via a loud speaker hookup*

I knew the mayor wanted Roosevelt, and what he wanted he got from me and the boys all the time. Boy, we had power that night. It scares me now to think about it.

> THOMAS GARRY, *the "voice from the sewer,"*
> *reminiscing about that historic night, 1976*

It's only when I became a politician [that] I lost my way.

> JAMES DVORAK, *former Chicago*
> *police officer and undersheriff*
> *of Cook County, sent to prison*
> *in 1994 for soliciting bribes*

The Philosophy of Mathias "Paddy" Bauler, Saloon Keeper and Alderman of the Forty-Third Ward from 1933 until 1967

Sit down! You look like a federal grand jury.

> *To a gathering of citizens*
> *who had come to hear him speak*

Chicago ain't ready for reform.

> *On the election of*
> *Mayor Richard J. Daley in 1955*

Them new guys in black suits and white shirts and narrow ties, them Ivy League types, them goo-goos. They think the whole thing is on the square.

You newspaper guys, don't you take anybody's hat and coat when you leave. I don't want to get sued.

Think of all those hangers-on who will be left homeless.

On closing his saloon at
403 North Avenue, September 9, 1960

What's it all mean? Nuttin. All you get out of it all is a few laughs.

■ ■ ■

The Bauler philosophy must never be accepted as representative of Chicago.

> Chicago Sun-Times
> *editorial, April 7, 1955*

I am a citizen of no mean city.

> ALDERMAN LEON DESPRES,
> *quoting Saint Paul of Tarsas, 1965*
> Acts 21.39

Look at Trenton, New Jersey; New York; and Philadelphia. What makes Chicago seem different is not the political corruption. It is a continuation of our aura as a town run by criminals with political connections, a holdover from the Al Capone era. You mention Chicago to a foreigner, and they don't ask you about the Impressionists at the Art Institute.

> TWENTIETH WARD ALDERMAN CLIFFORD
> KELLEY, *convicted on corruption charges*

I'm not right all the time, just ninety-nine times out of a hundred.

> VITO MARZULLO, *former*
> *Twenty-Fifth Ward alderman*

[Richard J.] Daley wanted power, and I wanted money. We both got what we wanted.

> THOMAS KEANE, *floor leader in the*
> *city council and former chairman of*
> *the Finance Committee, indicted on*
> *seventeen counts of mail faud and sen-*
> *tenced to five years in prison in 1974*

So I have relatives on the payroll. They're doin' an excellent job, so what?

> FORMER FIRST WARD ALDERMAN FRED ROTI,
> *convicted of soliciting bribes during the*
> *Operation Gambat investigation, 1989*

"Fast Eddie"

Former Tenth Ward alderman and talk show host
Edward Vrdolyak was leader of the Vrdolyak 29 faction
that opposed Mayor Harold Washington in the 1980s

It's the party of the liberals and the left wingers and the kooks and the crazies who have lost sight of Middle America.

VRDOLYAK *on the Democratic Party*

Always, no matter what you've got, stand up—be a man—be a *mensch*.

I'm not the kind of guy you tell "Go sit in the corner" and I just go sit there. That's not how I got where I got. I've worked for a lot of mayors. I've been elected a lot of times, and lemme tell you this, don't try to take away my method. Because you can't. Because nobody, I mean nobody, can blow me off like this.

This is it, isn't it? You bet it is. The game's afoot, baby!

■ ■ ■

Harold Washington, Chicago's first
African-American mayor, 1983–87, on "Fast Eddie"

I've known guys like Eddie all my life. I grew up with them. He's not a racist. He's a bully. He'll use race. Hell, he'll use anything. He'll use his own grandmother to get what he wants. But that doesn't make him a bad guy in my book. Amoral, yes; racist, uh-uh.

■ ■ ■

Power breeds arrogance, and arrogance, of course, breeds corruption, and there has been too much of both in Chicago.

VIRGIL PETERSON, *executive director*
of the Chicago Crime Commission, 1942

I love people that take dough, because you know exactly
where you stand.

> WAYNE OLSON, *former judge of the*
> *circuit court who was sentenced*
> *to twelve years in prison for bribery*
> *and racketeering, c. 1983*

Because so many of [the judges] have been aldermen, county
commissioners, or had other political jobs and offices, the fix
isn't foreign to them. So going on the bench means things
change only in that somebody no longer says, "Here's your
envelope, Alderman." Instead they say, "Here's your envelope, your Honor."

> MIKE ROYKO, *October 23, 1975*

Chicago justice is as real as foxfire—it glitters in the darkness
but only from a distance.

> OVID DEMARIS, *author*

To outsiders it can sound like a secret code, as when a pay-roller in City Hall says, "There was a beef from a goo-goo because I took a little fresh, and I was gonna get vised, but my clout squared it." Which of course means, "A reformer complained that I was taking bribes, and I was about to be fired, but my political sponsor hushed it up."

MIKE ROYKO, *June 7, 1973*

Never give an answer when you can reply with a question. Never say anything if you can wink. Never wink if you don't have to.

BILL REILLY, *Chicago raconteur,
with a credo for Windy City
politicians to live by*

The death of democracy is not likely to come by assassination from ambush. It will be a slow extinction from apathy, indifference, ignorance, and undernourishment.

ROBERT MAYNARD HUTCHINS, *former
president of the University of Chicago*

We don't want nobody ⟨THAT NOBODY⟩ sent. We don't want nobody who don't want no job. And we don't want nobody from the University of Chicago.

> *Words of ~~advice~~ REBUFF from a precinct captain*
> *to future Congressman Abner Mikva, 1948*

The contemplation of municipal corruption is gratifying to Chicagoans. They are helpless to do anything about it but they like to know it is on a grand scale. Ambivalence is a Chicago characteristic. People you meet at a party deal more time than people elsewhere to talking about good government, but they usually wind up the evening boasting about the high quality of crooks they have met.

> A. J. LIEBLING

Old age isn't for sissies.

> U.S. REPRESENTATIVE SIDNEY YATES,
> *at eight-five, announcing he will*
> *seek another term, 1995*

Quotes from Some of Chicago's Most Notable Chief Executives Whose Last Name Did Not Happen to Be Daley

William B. Ogden, Chicago's First Mayor, 1837–38

I was born close to a sawmill, was cradled in a sugar trough, christened in a mill pond, early left an orphan, and graduated from a log schoolhouse, and at fourteen found I could do anything I turned my head to and that nothing was impossible, and ever since . . . I have been trying to prove it with some success.

■ ■ ■

John Wentworth, Mayor of Chicago, 1857, 1860–61

I never did and never will live on time. Got no use for call bells, dinner bells, or alarm clocks. My doctrine is this: Eat when you're hungry, drink when you're thirsty, sleep when you're tired, and get up when you're ready.

If I get tired of laying on my back, I will have room to turn over and kick.

Explaining the need for
purchasing an oversized burial plot

Boys! This is the prince of Wales! He's come to see the city, and I'm going to show him around! Prince, these are the boys!

Introducing the sixteen-year-old Edward
VIII to the "boys," September 22, 1860

■ ■ ■

Carter Harrison I, Mayor of Chicago, 1879–86, 1893
They who think that the morals of a great crowded city can be made pure by law are as much dreamers as the mad anarchists who imagine that crime can be destroyed by killing law.

William Hale Thompson,
Mayor of Chicago, 1915–23, 1927–31
What was good enough for George Washington is good enough for Bill Thompson. I want to make the King of England keep his snoot out of America! America, first, last, and always!

William E. Dever, Mayor of Chicago, 1923–27

The wise legislator in a democracy will not attempt to impose a law, however desirable in the abstract, that will not receive general support of the people.

On the failures of the Volstead Act
to suppress alcohol consumption
and the criminal empire it spawned

Anton Cermak, Mayor of Chicago, 1931–33

I do not know whether I'm going to get well. I hope that whoever succeeds me will make his first duty the payment of money owed the teachers. If this will have helped me get loans, I'm glad I was shot. This bit of lead is not too burdensome for me to carry for a long time. I have had lead in my heart over their distress. Don't worry about me or whether I get well. I am sure I can suffer for the sake of Chicago, particularly when it spared the life of our greatest president to me.

Expressing concerns for the unpaid
Chicago schoolteachers hours after
being shot in the company of President-
elect Franklin D. Roosevelt in Miami,
Florida, February 15, 1933

■■■

Edward J. Kelly, Mayor of Chicago, 1933–47

All I have—what little I have—I got from the good people of Chicago.

To be a real mayor you've got to have control of the party. You've got to be a potent political figure. You've got to be a boss.

In politics the machine runs you, or you run the machine. I run the machine.

■■■

Martin Kennelly, Mayor of Chicago, 1947–55

Why live if you don't live in Chicago?

Crime syndicate? I don't know about any syndicate. Isn't that man Capone supposed to be dead?

■ ■ ■

Michael Bilandic, Mayor of Chicago, 1976–79

In the early history of Christianity you see a leader starting with twelve disciples. They crucify the leader and made martyrs of the others. And what was the result? Christianity is bigger and stronger than it was before.

Comparing his administration
to the sufferings of Christ

■ ■ ■

Jane Byrne, Mayor of Chicago, 1979–83

If we've got a lemon, I don't want to make lemonade. I'd rather just throw out the lemon.

The fear in this town can be terrible.

From now on everything that goes wrong, that's my baby. From now on it's all mine.

■ ■ ■

Harold Washington, Mayor of Chicago, 1983–87

We made the hard choices. We took the heat. And we changed the way the game is played.

I'm not a boss, and some people say that's a fatal flaw. I don't think so. I sleep at night.

You've had two kinds of mayors in this city. One who watered the machine, patted it, squeezed it, and milked it dry. The others were like me, trying to clean it up.

I don't know what it is I got, but the old ladies, they like me.

8

Our Daley Bread

Quotations from Chairman Richard & Son . . . and Those Who Knew Them Best

Richard J. Daley, Mayor of Chicago, 1955–76

On Daley
When you travel and you speak of Chicago, people say: "That is Mayor Daley's town!"

ALDERMAN THOMAS KEANE

Although he came up in politics as a product of the Democratic machine, [Richard J. Daley] has the intelligence and personal philosophy needed to take a broad view of community problems.

Chicago Sun-Times
editorial, April 7, 1955

Study the portrait of Mayor Richard J. Daley as you would a Rembrandt or a Goya. It's awesome, his startling resemblance to the Buddha. A touch of Gaelic perhaps, but God-like nonetheless. It bears a religious significance.

STUDS TERKEL, Talking to
Myself: A Memoir of My Times, *1977*

He talked to real people, not intellectuals or moralists. He cut through the distancing layers of political rhetoric which separate most elected officials from their constituents. Daley was the essence of all the people who live on the side streets of any great city, and he spoke to these people directly.

> FRANK SULLIVAN, *former press*
> *secretary to Richard J. Daley,* Legend

Richard J. Daley: In His Own Words
I'm not saying my party can't stand improving. Neither party has a monopoly on power.

April 3, 1955

"Boss" should apply to someone who unreasonably imposes his way. I thought I was the leader of the city. You don't call the leader of a church or synagogue "boss."

April 20, 1969

Robert's Rules of Order is the greatest book ever written.

October 3, 1967

There's no regard for the *Rules of Order* by the gentleman from the Fifth Ward. Go on with your disorder.

April 10, 1969

Look at Bridgeport . . . houses as old as on the West Side, but the people took care of them, worked hard, kept the neighborhood clean. Let me tell you something about those people. [African-Americans] should lift themselves up by their bootstraps like our grandparents did. Work hard, take care of their homes.

To a nun from the
Third Ward, mid-1960s

I don't know the facts, but I'll get them from experts.

February 14, 1968

I have lived in Chicago all my life, and I still say we have no ghettos in Chicago.

July 9, 1963

We hope by the end of 1967 we will have removed every slum and blight home in Chicago.

May 18, 1967

Chicago is the supermarket of the world.

August 13, 1956

Chicago is the melting pot of the nation.

May 11, 1960

I make no apologies to anyone for our great city.

February 8, 1964

It is amazing what they will be able to do once they get the atom harassed.

February 8, 1960

Ladies and gentlemen of the League of Women Voters . . .

December 1963

I resent the insinuendos.

May 15, 1965

Together we must rise to ever higher and higher platitudes.

March 13, 1967

All Republicans are funny.

October 2, 1967

There is nothing more immoral than a newspaperman. You ought to know, Frank. You were one of them.

To Frank Sullivan, his press secretary

They have vilified me. They have crucified me. Yes, they have even criticized me.

August 1968

Gentlemen, get one thing straight once and for all. The policeman isn't there to create disorder—the policeman is there to preserve disorder.

September 23, 1968

Our police are not all guilty of brutality.

February 10, 1969

Say That Again? Richard M. Daley, Mayor of Chicago, 1989–

I'm a proponent of cities going bankrupt.

To a Newsweek *reporter, 1992*

When you're celebrating in America, what you do is you break a window and grab something.

Following the riots
accompanying the second
Chicago Bulls championship, June 1992

Everybody's worried about apathy.

January 1996

When I give my word, it's my word. God always impressed me. I believe in God, but he doesn't have to worry about my word.

August 1995

The Bears are telling the people of Chicago and their fans, "We don't need you anymore. We can go to Alaska." He'd [Bears owner Mike McCaskey] better watch out, they'll put him on a train and send him out. The whole idea of sports franchises threatening the public—that's taking place all over the country. People get tired of it. No one likes threats. That is not the way to negotiate. His grandfather never negotiated that way.

August 1995

I don't think they can do it. Maybe the governor can. Maybe there's something down his sleeve. I want to look down there. I look down there a lot. There's nothing down there.

*On Governor Jim Edgar's claim that a
domed stadium could be built without
the General Assembly's approval, 1995*

Next year is going to be a very important day for us in Cook County.

January 1996

I flunked two bar exams. I did not like the results personally.

People are getting tired of the old Washington bureaucracy and the Washington red tape. The Republicans say this. The Democrats say that. They just want someone to come up and say, "This is it. Forget about the elephants and donkeys. Let's all get on both an elephant and a donkey and ride the same way."

January 1996

Rule it out! Rule it in! Whatever you want for your paper, I'll rule it out!

To a Chicago Sun-Times *reporter
concerning their coverage of the
1991 tax hike*

No one likes negative. One thing I found out is that negative is negative, and it doesn't say anything positive about the individual.

March 18, 1996

If a rat is on your sandwich, it would help to know it before.

To a Chicago Sun-Times *reporter, 1994*

You're walking down the street and a Rottweiler bites you . . . you know, in the face, and takes half your jaw or your child's jaw. I think maybe you should maybe be a little alarmed and concerned about it, don't you think so?

Concerning dog-owner
crackdown, September 1995

Look what they're doing outside the city. You can't even drive down a highway and see a cow anymore. You see a sign.

On the vanishing
agrarian ideal, March 1996

They always say, "Well, you're not as good as your dad." But I lead my own life. This is my life.

March 1996

New York got it. Why shouldn't we get it? We're centrally located. We got the hotels. We got the new stadium, things like that.

> *On securing the 1996 Democratic*
> *National Convention, July 20, 1994*

It's a fire! Why did the man take a cigarette? Why did he have tires? We have to ask that individual. Why did he do it? That's the question. Why was there an accident?

> *Assessing blame for a fatal high-*
> *rise apartment fire, January 1996*

They live in the Potomac. They swim in the Potomac. They'll die in the Potomac.

> *On Democrats in Washington*
> *who fail to pay attention to the*
> *national mood, April 1, 1995*

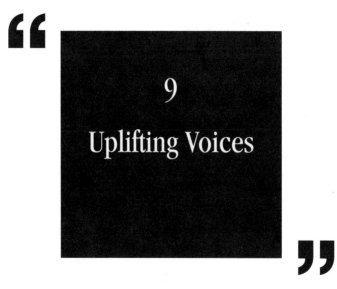

9

Uplifting Voices

■ ■ ■

In Chicago our God lurks everywhere. In the elevated train's husky roar. Beside the blinking lights of intensive care. In the clamor of the soybean trading floor, with those who suffer poverty and fright. In the humid mists of summer by the lake. On the Ryan through an icy night with a young widow weeping at a wake.

A city of beauty, hilarity and pain, boundless energy and permanent unrest. A terrifying, troubled hopeful place, its challenges intricate and arcane. Its opportunity . . . ah, the very best; to be an unclouded light of love and grace!

FATHER ANDREW GREELEY,
Andrew Greeley's Chicago

■ ■ ■

I am not orthodox about anything. I am thoroughly, completely, adequately, gloriously, and triumphantly a heretic.

DR. PRESTON BRADLEY, *founder of the*
People's Unitarian Church in Uptown

For Chicago I have nothing but the dearest love. It was the place of my birth into the kingdom of God—where I signed up with Jesus Christ as my manager for life. It was where I got into the biggest league of them all, the league where I will fight with the last drop of my blood until the great umpire says, "Bill, you're out!"

> EVANGELIST BILLY SUNDAY *played outfield*
> *for the Chicago White Stockings before*
> *his conversion to 'ol time religion.*

Cardinal Quotes

Patrick Cardinal Feehan,
Archbishop of Chicago, 1880–1902

The kingdom of heaven is like a grain of mustard seed, which a man took and sowed in his field, which is the least indeed of all seeds; but when it is grown up, it is greater than all herbs and becometh a tree. So that all the birds of the air come and dwell in the branches thereof.

> ARCHBISHOP FEEHAN'S *installation*
> *address at Holy Name Cathedral,*
> *November 25, 1880*

I know in whom I believed and trusted—*Scio Cui Credidi.*

Motto of ARCHBISHOP FEEHAN

George Cardinal Mundelein,
Archbishop of Chicago, 1916–39

Selfish employers of labor have flattered the Church by calling it the great conservative force, and then called upon it to act as a police force while they paid but a pittance of wages to those who worked for them. I hope that day is gone by. Our place is beside the poor, behind the working man. They are the people.

■ ■ ■

John Cardinal Cody,
Archbishop of Chicago, 1965–82

It is a basic tenent of our Catholic faith that discrimination on the basis of race, creed, or national origin is contrary to the will of God and unworthy of a follower of Jesus Christ.

As a religious leader I am obligated to speak out on moral and ethical issues that are often at the heart of political problems.

We used to say that when the Saints ran the Church, the Church was in bad condition.

On the archbishop as business manager

I am a Christian, a bishop, a person.

I wouldn't say that I have a best friend. I wouldn't say that I had any truly close friends, though. I don't have time.

My weakness is in that while I am doing the best I can, I cannot change either the wills of the hearts of those who harbored and seemingly acted out malicious designs against me. My infirmity is that in these relationships I cannot restore peace.

Final message to Chicago's Catholic
community and to all those who
opposed him through the years, 1982

He was not only the spiritual leader of the largest archdiocese in the nation, but he was a religious shepherd and friend to millions in Illinois. To many, John Cardinal Cody was a religious lighthouse during troubled times—he gave of himself for the good of his God, his Church, and his people.

GOVERNOR JAMES R. THOMPSON,
eulogizing Cardinal Cody, April 26, 1982

■ ■ ■

Joseph Cardinal Bernardin, Archbishop of Chicago, 1982–

The separation of church from state has been good for this country. But separation of church and state by the Constitution doesn't mean that there is no relationship between church and state; that somehow the state is to be totally secular.

I must be a man of hope. Without hope I might as well resign.

Let's get on with it.

> *To his doctors before*
> *undergoing cancer surgery*

The cardinal's mansion on Chicago's North State Parkway is a monument to Church triumphalism. It symbolizes an era that saw an immigrant church come out from under the hand of Know-Nothings and the American Protective Association to become a major power. Built in 1885 by Archbishop Patrick Feehan (1880–1902), it represented a church that was flexing its muscle in a city that was growing as fast as it could find immigrant bricklayers. During his twenty-two years as archbishop Feehan opened 119 parishes. It's entirely possible that Joseph L. Bernardin will also be archbishop for twenty-two years, during which time he might be forced to close 119 parishes.

> TIMOTHY UNSWORTH, *editor of*
> *the* U.S. Parish, *author of*
> The Last Priests in America, *1991*

■ ■ ■

You can never stop loving until the very end, because your last breath may be your best act of love.

Don't be afraid to stand up against injustices, whether it be in government, industry, in labor throughout the world. The injustice you find within yourself are also within the Church. Injustice weighs heavily upon personhood and denies the magnificence of almighty God.

> MONSIGNOR JOHN JOSEPH "JACK" EGAN, *director of the Office of Urban Affairs for the Chicago archdiocese. Monsignor Egan marched with the Reverend Ralph Abernathy in Selma, Alabama, in 1965 during the height of the civil rights movement.*

■ ■ ■

America has been undergoing some sort of religious revival but one that has not led to prosperity for most of the denominations.

> MARTIN MARTY, Where the Spirit Leads

I will give you a million dollars if you give me five years of your life.

> PHILIP DANFORTH ARMOUR *to the*
> *Reverend Frank Gunsaulus, pastor*
> *of Plymouth Congregational Church,*
> *who had just delivered the sermon*
> *"If I Had a Million Dollars," 1887*

I thank God that I am living in this day and in Chicago . . . our gospel is the only hope of the drunkard, the gambler, the harlot, the outcast, the despairing, the lost on the streets of Chicago. Oh, let us go and save them! Let us stretch our hands and keep them from pushing into the pit.

> DWIGHT LYMAN MOODY, *founder of the*
> *Moody Bible Institute, speaking at the*
> *Central Music Hall, September 16, 1893*

Social work means working for society, and society is a God-oriented affair.

> FATHER FREDERIC SIEDENBURG *established*
> *the Loyola School of Sociology in 1914,*
> *the first Catholic institution of its kind*
> *in the United States*

Reverend David Swing, Pastor
of the Chicago Central Church

In 1874 a Presbyterian journal accused the
Reverend Swing of preaching heresy. A trial took place,
but Swing was ultimately acquitted of all charges.

Man in his highest form must be a ceaseless action. His religion must be simple in creed but rich in activity.

It is not always the grandest sounds that are the soonest heard.

Civilization is more of the heart than mind.

True greatness never reveals nor cherishes much ambition, for the gift of mind and the possession of a profound character leave little for the soul to wish or for Earth to care for.

God has in no way connected human greatness with a ballot box.

■■■

In the midst of this busy material life of our day, art may call upon us to halt and turn our thoughts away from so much that is of the earth . . . and lead us to contemplate those eternal truths which after all most concern the children.

> CHARLES L. HUTCHINSON, *financier who founded the Art Institute of Chicago just six years out of high school*

If our plaster creations serve to set people to talking . . . to discussing, to considering in any way, to recognizing the possibilities of beauty in a commercial city, they will repay again.

> LORADO TAFT, *sculptor, dedicating*
> *ten nude statues to the Art Institute,*
> *June 16, 1899*

Whatever material wealth we have been given was given to us by the Lord to be used for his best purpose.

> NAOMI ANN DONNELLEY, *wife of Richard R.*
> *Donnelley, founder of R. R. Donnelley*

The generations to come will care nothing for our warehouses, our buildings, or our railroads, but they will ask, "What has Chicago done for humanity? Where has it made man wiser or nobler or stronger? What new thought or principles or trust has it given to the world?"

> JOHN PETER ALTGELD, *governor of*
> *Illinois, 1893–97, Academy of*
> *Science dedication speech, 1893*

The dignity of human persons also requires that every man enjoy the right to act freely and responsibly . . . this is to be done in such a way that each one acts on his own decision of set purposes, and from a consciousness of his obligation.

FATHER ANDREW GREELEY

I am a butcher trying to go to heaven.

PHILIP DANFORTH ARMOUR

And, finally, please God, give faith to those of us who lack it and help preserve the faith of those who are blessed with it.

JOHN CALLAWAY, *television talk show host and author,* The Thing of It Is, *1994*

"

10

**The Social
Conscience
of a City**

"

Sunday morning is a hangover in Chicago, even if you've never had a drop. The streets are empty of people, littered with the debris of all the years that came up to this moment. The city has no gay lights for Sunday morning. Everything is seen as it really is: the shabby, graffiti-stained buildings, the rusting hulks of dead cars squatting on flat tires at curbside, and old newspapers and Big Mac wrappers blowing in the sudden gusts of breeze that come around the corners like muggers. I always liked Sunday morning before I got married.

BILL GRANGER, Chicago Pieces

Knowledge is not the highest of the intellectual goods. Of higher value is understanding and, beyond that, wisdom.

DR. MORTIMER ADLER, *director of the Institute for Philosophical Research,* Ten Philosophical Mistakes, *1985*

A Republican is a man who wants you to go to church every Sunday. A Democrat says if a man wants to have a glass of beer he can have it.

"BATHHOUSE" JOHN COUGHLIN

Perhaps even in those first days we made a beginning toward the object which was afterward stated in our charter: "To promote a center for a higher civic and social life, to institute and maintain educational and philanthropic enterprises, and to investigate and improve the conditions in the industrial districts of Chicago."

JANE ADDAMS, *Nobel Prize winner*
and cofounder of Hull-House,
Twenty Years at Hull-House, *1910*

Jane Addams too knew that Chicago's blood was hustler's blood. Knowing that Chicago, like John the Baptist and "Bathhouse" John, like Bill Sunday and "Big Bill" Thompson, forever keeps two faces, one for winners and one for losers, one for hustlers and one for squares.

NELSON ALGREN,
Chicago: City on the Make

This is a frontier town. And it's got to go through its red-blooded youth. A church and a WCTU never growed a big town yet.

GEORGE WELLINGTON "CAP" STREETER

Drink and tobacco are the great separatists between men and women, but women's evolution has carried her beyond them.

FRANCES WILLARD, *founder of
the Women's Christian Temperance
Union in Evanston*

A lot of real Chicago lives in the neighborhood taverns—it is the mixed German and Irish and Polish gift to the city, a bit of the old country grafted into a strong new plant in the new.

BILL GRANGER, *1983*

Eyewitnesses to Chicago History

Haymarket, May 4, 1886

The names of August Spies, A. R. Parsons, and Sam Fielden, the blatant blatherskites who incited a mob of half-brained anarchists to shoot down forty or more police officers Tuesday night with a dynamite bomb and with revolvers, were on every lip yesterday. When citizens received their morning papers containing accounts of the cowardly assassination and the bloody battle which followed, they were thunderstruck. Hundreds of businessmen repaired to the City Hall to consult with Chief of Police Ebersold and Mayor Harrison before going to their places of business to insist upon the immediate apprehension and arrest of all of [the] fiends who incited the murder.

Chicago Tribune, *May 6, 1886*

Eyewitnesses to Chicago History

Haymarket, May 4, 1886 Continued

There will be a time when our silence will be more powerful than the voices you hear today.

> AUGUST SPIES, *newspaper publisher and labor leader, executed with Albert Parsons, George Engel, and Adolph Fischer on November 11, 1887, for their role in the Haymarket bombing*

Hurrah for anarchy! This is the happiest moment of my life.

> GEORGE ENGEL, *last words on the gallows*

Will I be allowed to speak? O men of America? Let me speak, Sheriff Matson! Let the voice of the people be heard!

> ALBERT PARSONS, *last words on the gallows*

Eyewitnesses to Chicago History

Haymarket, May 4, 1886 Continued

The law is vindicated.

> CHICAGO POLICE INSPECTOR
> MICHAEL SCHAAK, *November 11, 1887,*
> *moments after the "drop"*

The anarchists will understand they cannot do as they please in this country.

> POLICE CHIEF FREDERICK EBERSOLD,
> *in reply*

If I talked as radical as I feel, I could not be where I am.

> GOVERNOR JOHN PETER ALTGELD *par-*
> *doned the imprisoned Haymarket*
> *anarchists on June 26, 1893, and was*
> *damned for it*

Eyewitnesses to Chicago History

Haymarket, May 4, 1886 Continued

He was ever a friend of the common people, and his heart was ever full of sympathy for the poor, the lowly, and the oppressed. His vigorous voice and powerful pen were ever at the disposal of this class of his fellow citizens.

MAYOR EDWARD DUNNE, *funeral eulogy for John Peter Altgeld, September 6, 1915*

Chicago, city of our Black Friday [Haymarket Riot], cause of my rebirth. Next to Pittsburgh, it was the most ominous and depressing to me.

EMMA GOLDMAN, *anarchist*

■ ■ ■

I was born an anarchist. I was always against things. Sometimes I guess, I was even against myself.

> DR. BEN REITMAN, *founder of*
> *the Hobo College of Chicago*
> *and Emma Goldman's lover*

From ten to twenty I traveled in boxcars, ships, walked along highways thinking, dreaming, planning about building a better world. I had never been educated, had read little, was without a religion, culture, or a behavior pattern. I developed as "topsy," a natural anarchist; had no standards, ideals, or goals. Just wanted to live and learn how to help others do the same and be happy.

> *Comments made on*
> *January 1, 1939, his sixtieth birthday*

■ ■ ■

Ben Reitman represented the type of philosopher that gives the sweet, intoxicating drink of hope to the needy, thirsty, starving pedestrian prodding down the dusty road of life.

CON MAN JOSEPH "YELLOW KID" WEIL,
eulogizing Ben Reitman, 1942

Saul Alinsky, Activist and Founder of the Back-of-the-Yards Neighborhood Council

Change comes from power, and power comes from organization. In order to act, people must get together.

The haves made the laws. The have-nots must appeal to a higher law.

You can't compromise on the basic principles of a free and open society.

Life is too short not to be full of passion and commitment.

The meatpacking industry has never been able to distinguish between a Hereford steer and a human being.

The only place where you really have consensus is where you have totalitarianism.

As you know I have some rather unorthodox standards and one of them is the valuing of friendship above any of the other things people regard as treasures.

■ ■ ■

He was a true liberal with a love of freedom and a respect for the individual.

> MONSIGNOR JOHN "JACK" EGAN, *director of Urban Affairs for the Chicago archdiocese, on Saul Alinsky, 1972*

Chicago, August 1968

This is the most amazing thing that has ever occurred in the Loop of Chicago in modern history. A firecracker went off there. They have just turned Michigan and Balbo into a war zone. They have cleared part of the intersection. They have young people off on the sidewalk now. I have seen dozens of them being beaten, and the police really mean business here in front of the Hilton Hotel. "The whole world watches, the whole world watches," they are shouting. The police are regrouping. The whole world watches.

> *Contemporary news account of*
> *the street rioting outside the*
> *Hilton Hotel during the 1968*
> *Democratic National Convention*

Someday a mob may come into your town, come down your streets, and you will want your police department to stand its ground the way the Chicago police department did.

> FRANK SULLIVAN, *in defense of*
> *the Chicago Police Department*

. . . National conventions are games of a sort, and sports offer few spectacles richer in low comedy . . . It is sadly different this week in the police state which Richard (the Lion Hearted) Daley has made of the city he rules. There is no room for laughter in the city of fear.

> RED SMITH, *nationally syndicated*
> *sports columnist, on the "Siege*
> *of Chicago," 1968*

We were aware . . . that Chicago was, in some topsy-turvy way, the largest southern town in America. Shoot-to-kill Daley made it known at every turn that he played a rough-and-tumble game . . . One could not naively venture into Chicago expecting hearts and flowers. When the breakdown of negotiations made it clear the city would force a confrontation, we knew only the bravest of our generation would answer the call.

> YIPPIE LEADER ABBIE HOFFMAN'S
> *reflections on the 1968 Democratic*
> *Convention,* Soon to Be a Major
> Motion Picture, *1980*

Thinkers

My object in the world is to think new thoughts.

EDITH ROCKEFELLER MCCORMICK

For a century everything came easily to Chicago. We were halfway to everywhere.

MARTIN E. MARTY, *University of Chicago theologian, author of forty-five books, and editor of the* Christian Century

Preparation for the duties of citizenship is one of those objectives of any sound system of public schooling in our society. Preparation for earning a living is another, and the third is preparation for discharging everyone's moral obligation to lead a good life and make as much of one's self as possible. Our present system of compulsory basic schooling, kindergarten through twelfth grade, does not serve any of these objectives well.

DR. MORTIMER ADLER

History suggests that capitalism is a necessary condition for political freedom. Clearly it is not a sufficient condition.

> DR. MILTON FRIEDMAN,
> *University of Chicago*
> *economist and Nobel Prize winner*

The purpose of science is to extend our knowledge of forces of nature. The whole history of civilization is witness to the compelling necessity of this process. Any danger to mankind lies in the destructive use of discoveries which could have been used for its benefit. It does not lie in the discoveries themselves.

> ENRICO FERMI, *physicist. On December 2, 1942, Fermi and other members of the Manhattan Project achieved the first controlled nuclear reaction at the University of Chicago.*

It seems that in politics as in religion action will only follow conversion.

> HENRY J. HYDE, *U.S. congressman*

The true measure of a human is how he or she treats his fellow man. Integrity and compassion cannot be learned in college, nor are these qualities inherited in the genes.

> ESTHER PAULINE FRIEDMAN (ANN LANDERS),
> *whose advice column debuted in the*
> Chicago Sun-Times *on October 16, 1955*

In the history of the world the poets will be remembered more than the practical men, but actual life is made by the practical men, inspired at times by the writings of the dreamers.

> SIDNEY HILLMAN, *labor organizer*

Eternal vigilance is the price of liberty, and it does seem to me that notwithstanding all those social agencies and activities, there is not that vigilance which should be exercised in the preservation of our rights.

> IDA B. WELLS, *social reformer*
> *and civil rights crusader*

■ ■ ■

A slum develops any place where the people who reside in the area have not control of the economic resources over the political decisions which affect their lives.

You may be born in the slum, but the slum is not born in you.

We have the right to be wealthy, not just to get jobs. We [already] had a full-time employment thing—slavery.

REVEREND JESSE JACKSON

■ ■ ■

Your "I Will" is more important than your IQ.

MARVA COLLINS, *West Side educator and a philosophy to live by*

If we can break the backbone of discrimination in Chicago, we can do it in all the cities of this country.

> REVEREND DR. MARTIN LUTHER KING, JR.
> *during his visit to Chicago, 1966*

I believe you have no reason to take up space on the earth unless you have a purpose. And all of us have a purpose; to do what you can while you can for mankind.

> NANCY B. JEFFERSON, *African-American*
> *activist, often called the Mother Teresa*
> *of the West Side*

11

Meet the Press

*Voices of
Chicagoland Media*

Our aim: To fear God, tell the truth, and make money.

> H. C. PADDOCK, *publisher and founder*
> *of the suburban* Paddock *newspapers*

■ ■ ■

It is a newspaper's duty to print news and raise hell.

> WILBUR F. STOREY,
> *publisher of the* Chicago Times

If the *Times* is not allowed to publish, there will be no *Tribune*.

> *June 2, 1863, after Union Army General*
> *Ambrose Burnside ordered the* Times
> *closed because of its Copperhead, or*
> *pro-Southern, pro-slavery, sympathies.*
> *The paper reopened a day later.*

■ ■ ■

■ ■ ■

The saddest day for Chicago newspapers was when they started taking politicians seriously and reporting their everyday doings and sayings.

Chicago is a sort of journalistic Yellowstone Park—offering haven to a last herd of fantastic bravos.

I have lived in other cities but been inside only one. I knew Chicago's thirty-two feet of intestines. Only newspapermen ever achieve this bug-in-a-rug citizenship.

BEN HECHT

■ ■ ■

One of the things a newspaper can never hope to do is convince its readers that nobody beats the odds but the oddsmakers.

HENRY JUSTIN SMITH,
journalist and author

Before I started my life's work—journalism—I was counseled by my beloved father that a good newspaper was one of the best instruments of service and one of the strongest weapons ever to be used in defense of a race which was deprived of its citizenship rights.

> ROBERT S. ABBOTT *founded the* Chicago Defender *in 1905. His newspaper beckoned thousands of African Americans caught in the daily grind of southern segregation to abandon the Jim Crow South and come to Chicago.*

You've got to love a town to be a reporter in it, and, babe, I don't love.

> CHARLES MACARTHUR *co-wrote* The Front Page *and other screenplays with Ben Hecht*

We are not literary men in this room but the dregs of journalism. Some of us can barely read.

> *City Hall press room reporter*

■ ■ ■

The purpose of a newspaper is to print gossip that's true.

The reporters today are frustrated F.B.I. agents. The newspapers are highbrow, elitist, overly adversarial, and preachy.

> Jay McMullen, *former*
> Chicago Sun-Times *reporter,*
> *later married to Mayor Jane Byrne*

■ ■ ■

I've reported murders, scandals, marriages, premieres, and national political conventions. I've been amused, intrigued, outraged, enthralled, and exasperated by Chicago. And I've come to love this American giant, viewing it as the most misunderstood, most underrated city in the world. There is none other quite like my City of Big Shoulders.

> Irv Kupcinet *began Kup's Column in 1941.* Kup's Chicago, *1962*

■ ■ ■

All shades of opinion, all significant versions of the facts should have representation and be given free access to the channels of communication.

> MARSHALL FIELD III,
> *publisher of the defunct* Chicago Sun

If the radicals are right and everything I do will be shaped by my own self-interest, why listen to conscience?

> JACK FULLER, *president and*
> *publisher of the* Chicago Tribune, *1996*

Chicago Newspaper Mottos

With drips of ink, we make millions think.

> Chicago Defender

A Paper for People Who Think

Chicago Herald & Examiner *motto, 1930s*

Independent in Nothing, Republican in Everything

Chicago Inter-Ocean, *1870s*

The Independent Newspaper

Chicago Daily News, *1970s*

An American Paper for the American People

Chicago American, *1950s*

The Bright One!

Chicago Sun-Times, *1970s*

The World's Greatest Newspaper

Chicago Tribune *motto, coined in 1911*

■ ■ ■

The *Tribune* has come out against syphilis. Bet you 8-5 syphilis'll win.

Anonymous, 1940

A mind that considers movies only at review length will atrophy.

ROGER EBERT, *Pulitzer Prize-winning film critic for the* Chicago Sun-Times

Hollywood premieres black action, sex, and violence in Chicago. That's what they think of the mass taste in Chicago.

GENE SISKEL, Chicago Tribune *film critic, began reviewing movies in September 1969*

An advocate's role is to be an advocate. My role is to report on what the advocate is saying.

NBC-TV news anchor
CAROL MARIN, *May 23, 1996*

So why have I lasted so long? Because I'm the best damn rock 'n 'roll disc jockey that's ever lived . . . that's why! I often say on the air that I'm not conceited or egotistical. I am just plain fantastic! I admit that it's possible to think you're good and be wrong, but it's impossible to be good and know you are, and I know I'm the best.

LARRY LUJACK, *king of the*
rock 'n' roll deejays, Superjock, *1975*

My father died when I was eight, so I was a Depression baby without a daddy or a hero. But if I had to put a hero together from that period, it would be someone who could think like Einstein, could hit a baseball like Ruth, and had the guts of Lindbergh.

WALLY PHILLIPS, *WGN-radio talk*
show host, on heroes and role models

Today there's no romance in the business anymore—no glamor. In my day we had romance. Rough but good times.

> WALTER SPIRKO, *dean of*
> *city police reporters, 1993*

I sometimes get kind of Dick and Jane-ish in some of my stories. But it's Dick and Jane that most people understand.

> WALTER JACOBSON, *former Chicago*
> *Cubs batboy turned investigative reporter*
> *for the* Chicago American, *WBBM-TV,*
> *and WFLD-FOX 32*

At night when people called in, I would always ask them where they were. They were alone. Alone at work. Alone in the cab of their truck. Alone in the kitchen. Alone in bed. Alone . . . except for the radio. Being alone, they wanted a bond with other people, and you gave it to them. You became their friend.

> EDDIE SCHWARTZ, *all-night talk*
> *show host with WIND, WGN, and WLUP*

It is entirely possible for me to be a biased reporter. I struggle against it every day. But it is also possible to be a biased viewer.

CAROL MARIN

Some women don't want an aggressive self-image. I don't mind being thought of as a cold-hearted, tough bitch. There were many years when I was intimidated by men in three-piece suits and buffed nails. I can be damned intimidating myself now.

SUSAN ANDERSON, *the first female general assignment reporter on WBBM-TV, on women in the newsroom, 1977*

We're just messengers . . . At our best, we're just messengers.

CAROL MARIN, *May 23, 1996*

Then stand to your glasses steady
And drink to your comrade's eyes
Here's a toast to the dead already
And hurrah for the next who dies

> *Ghoulish drinking song popularized*
> *by Chicago reporters at the*
> *Whitechapel Club, 173 Calhoun Place*

12

Performing Arts

Entertainment in Chicago

A good picture must be in a worthy frame.

> MARY GARDEN, *operatic star*
> *born in Aberdeen, Scotland,*
> *but raised in Hyde Park*

A long slow lift of that white arm and she has portrayed ecstasy.

> Chicago Tribune, *on a*
> *performance by Mary Garden, 1921*

Something extraordinary happened in Chicago. I made no changes. We didn't have to adjust to each other. Our ways of making music were the same. Wine became champagne; we sparkle together. It's like Siegfried and Brunhilde. The girl was beautiful, and Siegfried turned out not to be impotent.

> SIR GEORG SOLTI, *maestro of the*
> *Chicago Symphony Orchestra,*
> *on coming to Chicago*

I don't like opera. What's it all about anyway?

Anonymous Chicago stockbroker, 1921

Chicago was a good town to grow up in, with the exception of an unfortunate element that plagued the entire community: organized crime. The mob, or whatever you want to call it, was a fact of life in the Chicago of the 1920s. Some guys became gangsters through greed, some through necessity.

FRANKIE LAINE, *pop balladeer*
born in Little Italy in 1913,
started singing at Chicago's
North Side nightclubs in the 1930s

There was no need to inform us of the protocol involved. We were from Chicago and knew all about cement.

GROUCHO MARX, *pressing his hands into*
the cement at Graumann's Chinese The-
ater in Hollywood. The Marx Brothers
lived at 4649 Calumet Avenue in 1910.

In 1938 when I was attending Hyde Park High School, my attendance record was nothing to be proud of. Some mornings when I got off the streetcar at 62nd Street and Stony Island Avenue, the park across the street from the school proved such an irresistible temptress that instead of going to class, I'd strike off through the trees and spend the whole day walking along the windy lakefront or wandering through the enormous halls of the Museum of Science and Industry or sitting in the grass writing poetry.

> STEVE ALLEN, *comedian, author, and the original host of the* Tonight Show

I was taken out of the sticks and a poor environment and thrust into a wealthy suburb of Chicago and sent to this very sophisticated school called New Trier High where all the kids had cars and everything they wanted. The effect was to make me feel inferior. That was the beginning of my wanting to win at everything I ever took on. I get my drive, if you call it that, from that adolescence. I want to win, and I always have since those days back in high school.

> CHARLTON HESTON, *1976*

As I peeled away the layers of my life, I realized that all my craziness, all my pain and difficulties, stemmed from me not valuing myself.

OPRAH WINFREY, *1993*

I was happy at heart for out of the trouble and confusion stood a mocking, merry little figure. Vague and indefinite at first, but it grew and grew and grew and finally arrived—a little mouse. A romping, rollicking little mouse. The idea completely engulfed me. The wheels turned to the tune of it—"chug, chug—mouse—chug, chug—mouse," the train seemed to say. The whistle screeched it. A "mm--ouuse" it wailed. By the time my train had reached the middle west I had dressed my dream mouse in a pair of red velvet pants and two huge pearl buttons and employed the first scenario and was all set.

WALT DISNEY, *born at 2156 Tripp Avenue in Chicago, describing the birth of Mickey Mouse on board a train.*

When I was a kid, Glenda the Good Witch of the North in *The Wizard of Oz* was my heroine.

> JANE PAULEY, *news anchor on WMAQ-TV,*
> *who later hosted the* Today Show

Maybe I just need a lot of men admiring me, because when I was a kid I never even had a date to the high school prom.

> KIM NOVAK, *actress, grew up in Chicago's*
> ~~*near western suburbs*~~ NORTHWEST SIDE

The fact that we can create the whole world with three chairs and a hat is incredible. The truly fascinating thing is to get an idea in the morning and see it on the stage in the evening filtered through the actors and the audience. Now that's going to be much more rewarding than Mork and Mindy.

> BERNARD SAHLINS, *founder of Second City,*
> *the pioneering repertory comedy*
> *company that spawned such stars as*
> *John and Jim Belushi, Elaine May,*
> *Mike Nichols, and George Wendt*

■ ■ ■

I could always make people laugh or frighten 'em or one or the other.

I don't know what it is to have a lot of ambition, except that you leave a trail of people you've hurt along the way. You never know what the end of ambition is anyway.

> JOHN BELUSHI, *comedian and star of* Animal House, *and a graduate of* Wheaton Central High

■ ■ ■

It was only after I got into acting that I started watching actors.

> GARY SINISE, *costar of* Forrest Gump *and a veteran of Chicago's Steppenwolf Theater, 1996*

I'm terribly chauvinistic about this city. Smell the air—it's sexy. Chicago is vital, and it continues to improve.

> LOIS NETTLETON, *actress,*
> *grew up in Oak Park, 1977*

I grew up in a world where all the images were white. God was white. All the people in power were men. Everybody at the Last Supper was a man. The Blessed Trinity was two men and a spirit. You can't come out of this experience not being a sexist and a racist. The show introduced me to Gloria Steinem and others who said things that were threatening because I knew they were talking about me.

> PHIL DONAHUE, *whose talk show*
> *originated in Chicago, 1977*

Chicago is a place to take risks, a place to fail, a place to grow. It's a place where you're not judged as being unworthy.

> WILLIAM L. PETERSEN, *film and*
> *television actor and cofounder*
> *of the Remains Theater*

I miss everything about Chicago, except January and February.

> GARY COLE, *television actor,*
> *star of* American Gothic *and*
> *other shows, and former member*
> *of Chicago's Remains Theater*

From the beginning my philosophy has been that people deserve to come and to leave [my show] with their dignity. I never did what you see on the air today . . . because I never wanted people to be humiliated and embarrassed.

> OPRAH WINFREY, *on the state of television*
> *talk shows in the '90s, July 1995*

If you're a star, you usually have a certain persona, and you're rarely able to break away from it. I'm not bound by any image. I just like to sort of blend in wherever I am.

> JOHN MAHONEY, *costar of*
> Frasier *and ensemble member*
> *of Steppenwolf Theater, 1994*

I've been a vagabond for a good part of my life, but when I get off the plane at O'Hare and come down the Kennedy . . . and I can see the city, I get comfortable.

WILLIAM L. PETERSEN, *1992*

The first thing I do when I get up in the morning is drop down on my knees and say a novena and a rosary. I'm the most fortunate guy in the world.

Movie tough guy DENNIS FARINA,
*former Chicago police officer
who grew up in the Old Town
neighborhood; costar of* Get Shorty,
Midnight Run, *and a featured actor
in numerous other films, 1996*

The greatest responsibility I feel is to my creator, and what I try to fulfill for myself is to honor the creation.

OPRAH WINFREY

I get bored out of my mind in Los Angeles. It's such an industry town. Here I have old friends who aren't in the business. I can walk to all sorts of good places where the waiters and waitresses don't want me to read their screenplays.

JOHN MAHONEY, *resident of Oak Park*

John Malkovich, Film and Theater Actor Who Got His Start at Steppenwolf Theater

I really prefer theater [to film] because you're in the flow. It's not removed. Theater is like life. You have to be there, while movies sort of tell you you can be there.

I would like to be a success with something that does not make me want to vomit all over the screening room after I've seen it.

Very little of what I've done has lived up to what I intended.

If someone tells you they like you for your work, it's easier to deal with than if they like you for some other reason.

I've always felt if you can't make money as an actor, you're either incredibly stupid or tragically unlucky.

When Jazz Was King

Chicago in the 1920s was an age that was here and gone. I'm lucky I heard it . . . It was an era. New Orleans players were coming up the river; everyone was here. Bix, Louis, Baby Dodds, Jimmie Noone—Chicago was the place.

ART HODES, *jazz pianist who played with all the great ones*

I've played everywhere, and I've never heard musicians swing as hard as they do in Chicago.

RED RODNEY, *jazz trumpeter, 1994*

It was an accident that swing and I were born and brought up side by side in New Orleans, traveled up the Mississippi together, and in 1922 were there in Chicago getting acquainted with the North and the North getting acquainted with us.

> LOUIS ARMSTRONG, *jazz trumpeter,*
> *came up from New Orleans in 1922*

If you just think about some of the great swingers, even those in Harlem, like Willie "the Lion" Smith, Fats Waller, Eubie Blake, James P. Johnson, Lucky Roberts—none of those guys ever saw the inside of the state of Louisiana, and yet we continue to want to give New Orleans the credit when the credit belongs to Chicago. Chicago is where jazz was developed and where it actually happened.

> BUD FREEMAN,
> The Autobiography of Black Jazz

I took my public school training in three jails and plenty of poolrooms. Next, to college in a gang of tea pads (marijuana dens), earned my Ph.D. in more creep joints and speakeasies and dance halls than the law allows.

MEZZ MEZZROW, *Prohibition-era jazz pianist,* Really the Blues

I don't have any great love for Chicago. What the hell, a childhood around Douglas Park isn't very memorable. I remember the street fights and how you were afraid to cross the bridge 'cause the Irish kid on the other side would beat your head in. I left Chicago a long time ago.

BENNY GOODMAN, *1976*

People who think in terms of a blue-collar sound when they think of Chicago jazz, you know—rollicking, honking jive—are missing the point. It's really sophisticated. It has to be to sound so relaxed.

JOEL SPENCER, *drummer, 1994*

Home of the Blues

The blues ain't nothin' but a good woman cryin' for a man.

Anonymous

If you don't dig the blues, you have a hole in your soul.

JIMMIE RODGERS, *blues guitarist*
and Chess Records recording artist

The blues is a road. All other music don't have no road, and once you step on that road, from that point on, you can't turn back. From that point on, you're livin' the life of a bluesman. As you become a man, a bluesman, you find that you can't work and play the blues. The true definition of a blues man is a black man, 30 to 40 to 70, livin', eatin', and playin' the blues for a living—no side gig, nothin'. That's the true definition. No other person in this world could be a blues man.

TRE HARDIMAN, *guitarist,*
on traditional Chicago blues

The blues don't always mean trouble and misunderstanding. The blues mean it's always better up the road.

> WILLIE DIXON, *session bassist,*
> *songwriter, record producer*

This is the crossroads of the United States—or should I say the world? There ain't nothin' that goes on nohow that don't come in here. This is where you find out what you want to find out any place, any time of the night. I came in 1941, and I won't live anyplace but Chicago.

> JUNIOR WELLS, *bluesman*

I just like them old blues. The reason I play 'em, I come up hard. I suffered 'em a lot of places. Person ain't never had no hard times, why, they don't know what the blues mean anyway. Take this young generation. They don't understand it. They're tryin' to learn it.

> HOWLIN' WOLF (CHESTER ARTHUR
> BURNETT) *came to Chicago in 1952*

We didn't know the South Side from the West Side. All these blues clubs had us goin' around in a circle. . . . There were a lot of blues clubs in kind of a circle. Tonight I would be at Sylvio's, Theresa's the next night, Mel's Hideaway the next night, and we just kept goin' around week after week, year after year. All of a sudden the 1960s came, and if you really want the truth, I think all of us around my age and maybe a little older came out of that style. Chess Records was here, and we got recorded and called it Chicago blues.

BUDDY GUY, *blues guitarist and owner of Buddy Guy's Legends nightclub*

It's no money in Chicago the way Chicago used to be. Chicago ain't hip no more.

SUNNYLAND SLIM (ALBERT LUANDREW), *pioneering 1950s blues pianist, speaking about the state of the blues in the 1970s*

They call me Muddy Waters. I'm just restless, man, as the deep blue sea.

> MUDDY WATERS (MCKINLEY
> MORGANFIELD), *blues guitarist*

[There] was so much racism in the North. When I was working in these factories and things, I heard these Polish cats and Hungarians or whatever they might be—immigrants you know. They came here to this paradise what my people took four hundred years without any kind of pay to make this rich paradise for them, and before the cat could speak well enough English to say his address correct, he was in the back there with the rest of those American white cats calling us niggers and things.

> EDDIE BOYD, *Delta bluesman, born
> in Clarksdale, Mississippi, began his
> recording career in Chicago in 1947*

Anywhere in the world you hear a Chicago bluesman play, it's a Chicago sound, born and bred.

> RALPH METCALFE, *U.S. congressman*

Index

■ ■ ■

Abbott, Robert S., 194

Adams, Charles Francis, 41

Adams, Franklin P., 97

Adams, Henry, 41

Addams, Jane, 175

Ade, George, 77, 85

Adler, Mortimer, 174, 186

Algren, Nelson, 84, 85, 88, 175

Alinsky, Saul, 182–83

Allen, Steve, 206

Altgeld, John Peter, 43, 111, 170, 180

Andersen, Arthur, 63

Anderson, Margaret, 14, 78, 90

Anderson, Sherwood, 77

Anderson, Susan, 201

Angell, George Thorndike, 5

Anonymous or unattributed quotations

on the blues, 217

from the *Chicago Inter-Ocean,* 43

Chicago proverb, 9

from the *Chicago Sun-Times,* 134, 148

from the *Chicago Times,* 36

from the *Chicago Tribune,* 177, 204

on the *Chicago Tribune,* 198

by a city employee, 126

from City Hall, 125
by a City Hall press room
　reporter, 194
from a Jackson, Michigan,
　newspaper, 2
by a *London Daily Mail*
　correspondent, 13
from a 1968 news account,
　184
Northwestern University
　halftime chant, 105
by a precinct captain, 140
by a stockbroker, 205
by a tour bus guide, 121
by a West Side alderman,
　125
Whitechapel Club drinking
　song, 203
by a youngster, to "Shoe-
　less" Joe Jackson, 95
Arden, Harvey, 21
Armour, Philip Danforth, 29,
　45, 51, 52, 167, 171
Armstrong, Louis, 215

Arpino, Gerald, 23
Arvey, Jake, 131
Asner, Ed, 20

Banham, Reyner, 18
Banks, Ernie, 98, 99
Barnes, Clive, 19
Barnett, Gary, 105
Bauler, Mathias "Paddy,"
　132–33
Baum, L. Frank, 79
Beaubien, Mark, 31
Beauvoir, Simone de, 17
Bellow, Saul, 84, 86
Belushi, John, 209
Bennett, Arnold, 12
Bernardin, Joseph Cardinal,
　164
Bernhardt, Sarah, 5
Bilandic, Michael, 145
Bismarck, Otto von, 4
the blues, 216–20
Borden, Mary, 11
Boyd, Eddie, 220

Bradley, Preston, 160
Bradwell, Myra Colby, 110
Bremer, Frederika, 3
Brennan, Bernard, 63
Brent, Stuart, 62, 89
Brickhouse, Jack, 92, 104
Brodsky, Stuart, 62, 89
Bross, William "Deacon," 37,
    39
Bryan, William Jennings, 42
Buck, Pearl S., 16
Burnett, Chester Arthur
    (Howlin' Wolf), 218
Burnett, Leo, 60, 61, 68
Burnham, Daniel, 48, 49
Butler, Michael, 66
Byrne, Jane, 145

Caldwell, Billy, 34
Callaway, John, 171
Capone, Al, 115–17
Caray, Harry, 92
Cartwright, Bill, 106
Casey, Jim, 122

Cermak, Anton, 143
Chamberlain, Everett, 35
Charles, Prince of Wales, 18
Chatfield-Taylor, Hobart C.,
    28, 44
Chesterton, G. K., 11
"Chicago" (song), 34
Chicago American motto, 197
Chicago Daily News motto,
    197
Chicago Defender motto, 196
Chicago Herald & Examiner
    motto, 196
Chicago Inter-Ocean motto,
    197
Chicago Sun-Times motto,
    197
Chicago Tribune motto, 197
Chirac, Jacques, 24
Cicotte, Ed, 94
Cody, John Cardinal, 162–64
Colander, Pat, 99
Colbert, Elias, 12, 35
Cole, Gary, 211

Collins, Marva, 189
Colvin, Harvey Doolittle, 4
Comiskey, Charles, 94
Cone, Fairfax, 61
Coughlin, "Bathhouse" John,
    127, 128, 174
Crane, Richard Teller, 50

Daley, Richard J., 126, 148–53
Daley, Richard M., 154–58
Daley, Steve, 92
Dana, Charles A., 40
Danforth, Philip, 169
Darrow, Clarence, 112
Dell, Floyd, 10, 81
Demaris, Ovid, 138
Democratic National Conven-
    tion (1968), 184–85
Despres, Leon, 134
Dever, William E., 143
Diana, Princess of Wales, 18
Dillinger, John, 120
Disney, Walt, 207
Ditka, Mike, 102

Dixon, Willie, 218
Donahue, Phil, 210
Donnelley, Naomi Ann, 170
Douglas, Paul H., 20
Dreiser, Theodore, 78, 110
Dunne, Edward, 180
Dunne, Finley Peter, 30
Durocher, Leo, 98
Dvorak, James, 132

The *Eastland,* 46
Ebersold, Frederick, 179
Ebert, Roger, 198
Egan, Msgr. John Joseph
    "Jack," 166, 183
Eisner, Michael D., 25
Elizabeth II, 17
Engel, George, 178
Everleigh, Minna, 110

Farina, Dennis, 212
Farrell, James T., 82
Feehan, Patrick Cardinal,
    161–62

Fermi, Enrico, 187
Fetzer, Herman, 11
Field, Eugene, 74, 82
Field, Marshall, I, 44
Field, Marshall, III, 196
Fiffer, Sharon Sloan, 89
Fischetti, John, 100
Fitzgerald, F. Scott, 77
Forster, E. M., 12
Freeman, Bud, 215
Friedman, Esther Pauline
    (Ann Landers), 188
Friedman, Milton, 187
Fuller, Henry Blake, 48, 76
Fuller, Jack, 196

Galvin, Paul, 60
Garden, Mary, 204
Garland, Hamlin, 80
Garry, Thomas, 131
Gates, John Warner, 51
Getzendanner, Susan, 113
Goddard, Connie, 89
Goldberg, Arthur J., 112

Goldblatt, Louis, 56, 62, 67
Goldman, Emma, 180
Goodman, Benny, 216
Grace, Mark, 99
Grange, Harold "Red," 101
Granger, Bill, 67, 174, 176
Great Chicago Fire, 35–38
Greeley, Fr. Andrew, 160, 171
Greene, Bob, 68, 70
Gregory, Dick, 129
Gunther, John, 121
Guy, Buddy, 219

Halas, George, 46, 100
Hardiman, Tre, 217
Harper, William Rainey, 107
Harrison, Carter, I, 142
Harte, Bret, 5
Haymarket, 177–80
Hecht, Ben, 74, 80, 193
Hefner, Hugh, 57-58
Helm, Margaret, 33
Hermann, Charles H., 129
Heston, Charlton, 206

Hillman, Sidney, 188
Hodes, Art, 214
Hoffman, Abbie, 185
Holmes, Oliver Wendell, 6
Hulbert, William, 108
Hull, Bobby, 95
Hutchins, Robert Maynard, 139
Hutchinson, Charles L., 169
Hyde, Henry J., 187

Insull, Samuel, 47, 49

Jackson, Rev. Jesse, 189
Jackson, Phil, 105, 107
Jacobson, Walter, 200
James, William, 74
jazz, 214–16
Jefferson, Nancy B., 190
Johnson, John H., 59, 62
Jordan, Michael, 106

Kaplan, Donna Lou (Sugar Rautbord), 71
Keane, Thomas, 135, 148

Keefe, John, 24
Kelley, Clifford, 134
Kelly, Edward J., 144
Kenna, Michael "Hinky Dink," 110, 128
Kennelly, Martin, 144
Kerfoot, William Dale, 38
Kimball, Harlow, 6
King, Rev. Martin Luther, Jr., 190
Kinzie, Juliette, 31
Kipling, Rudyard, 7, 38
Kupcinet, Irv, 195

Laine, Frankie, 205
Lardner, Ring, 85, 86, 93
La Salle, René-Robert Cavelier Sieur de, 2
Latrobe, Charles J., 32
Lawson, Victor, 75
Leonov, Major General Alexei A., 20
Levinson, Leonard Louis, 12
Liebling, A. J., 16, 76, 140
Lindsay, Vachel, 38

Lloyd, Henry Demarest, 30
Lorimer, George Horace, 87
Luandrew, Albert (Sunnyland Slim), 219
Lujack, Larry, 199
Lundin, Fred "The Poor Swede," 130

McAllister, Ward, 8
MacArthur, Charles, 194
MacArthur, John D., 65
McCaskey, Mike, 64
McCormick, Anne O'Hare, 15
McCormick, Chauncey, 86
McCormick, Cyrus Hall, 45, 52
McCormick, Edith Rockefeller, 186
McDonald, Michael Cassius, 114
McDowell, Jack, 97
McGurn, "Machine Gun" Jack, 119
McMullen, Jay, 195
Macrae, David, 4

MacVeigh, Franklin, 49
Mages, Morrie, 66
Mahoney, John, 211, 213
Mailer, Norman, 19
Malkovich, John, 213–14
Marin, Carol, 199, 201
Mark, Norman, 84
Marovitz, Abraham Lincoln, 111
Marquette, Fr. Jacques, 2
Marquis, Don, 14
Martin, William, 113
Martineau, Harriet, 3
Marty, Martin E., 166, 186
Marx, Groucho, 205
Marzullo, Vito, 135
Medill, Joseph, 37
Mencken, H. L., 10, 13, 16, 76
Menuhin, Yehudi, 22
Merriam, Charles, 124
Merriam, Robert E., 125
Metcalfe, Ralph, 220
Meyer, Ray, 104
Mezzrow, Mezz, 216
Mikan, George, 104

Minoso, Minnie, 94
Mr. Dooley, 30
Monroe, Harriet, 88
Montagu, Ashley, 21
Moody, Dwight Lyman, 167
Moran, George "Bugs," 118
Morganfield, McKinley
    (Muddy Waters), 220
Morris, Jan, 23
Morris, Jeannie, 103
Motley, Willard, 87
Mundelein, George Cardinal,
    162

Nettleton, Lois, 210
newspaper mottos, 198–99
Nixon, Richard M., 17
Nolan, William, 126
Norris, Frank, 79
Northwestern University half-
    time chant, 105
Novak, Kim, 208

O'Bannion, Dion, 118
O'Connor, Len, 126
O'Donnell, Edward "Spike,"
    117
Ogden, William B., 141
Oldenburg, Claes, 22
O'Leary, Catherine, 36
O'Leary, Jim, 114
Olson, Wayne, 138
O'Neill, Terence, 17
Owens, Jesse, 93

Paddock, H. C., 192
Paley, William S., 61
Palmer, Bertha Honore, 39,
    69
Palmer, Potter, 43
Panczko, Ed "Butch," 120
Panczko, Joseph "Pops," 121
Panczko, Paul "Peanuts," 121
Parsons, Albert, 179
Patterson, Joseph Medill, 50
Pauley, Jane, 208
Payton, Walter, 103

Peirce, Neal R., 24
Perry, George Sessions, 16
Petersen, William L., 210, 212
Peterson, Virgil, 137
Phillips, Wally, 199
Pokogon, Simon, 33
Pritzker, Abram Nicholas
    "A. N.," 56
Pritzker, Cindy, 70
Pritzker, Jay, 70
Pritzker, Robert, 64
Pullman, George, 48, 52, 71

Ralph, Julian, 40
Reilly, Bill, 139
Reinsdorf, Jerry, 96
Reitman, Ben, 181
Rodgers, Jimmie, 217
Rodman, Dennis, 107
Rodney, Red, 214
Rogers, Will, 130
Roosevelt, Franklin D., 15
Rosenwald, Julius, 53
Roti, Fred, 135

Royko, Mike, 82, 83, 124, 138,
    139
Rubloff, Arthur, 65, 66, 71
Runyon, Damon, 101
Rushdie, Salman, 23

Sahlins, Bernard, 208
Salenger, Lucy, 22
Sandburg, Carl, 81, 88, 113
Sayers, Gale, 102
Schaak, Michael, 179
Schliemann, Heinrich, 29
Schwartz, Eddie, 200
Shackleton, Robert, 14
Shaw, George Bernard, 7
Shepard, Jean, 95
Siedenburg, Fr. Frederic, 168
Sinclair, Upton, 30
Sinise, Gary, 209
Siskel, Gene, 198
Smith, Henry Justin, 193
Smith, Red, 185
Solti, Sir Georg, 206
Spencer, Joel, 216

Spies, August, 178
Spirko, Walter, 200
Stagg, Amos Alonzo, 103
Stead, William T., 8, 9, 42
Steevens, George, 9
Steffens, Lincoln, 8, 10
Stone, Melville, 75
Stone, W. Clement, 58, 62
Storey, Wilbur F., 192
Streeter, George Wellington
    "Cap," 115, 176
Sullivan, Frank, 149, 184
Sullivan, Louis Henri, 41, 47
Sunday, Billy, 161
Swift, Gustavus Franklin, 45,
    51
Swing, Rev. David, 168–69

Taft, Lorado, 87, 170
Talese, Gay, 21
Terkel, Studs, 83, 124, 148
Thompson, James R., 112,
    164

Thompson, William Hale,
    130, 142
Touhy, Roger, 119
Train, George Francis, 35
Twain, Mark, 7

Unsworth, Timothy, 165

Valukas, Anton, 124
Veblen, Thorsten, 52
Veeck, Bill, 96
Vrdolyak, Edward, 136–37

Walgreen, Charles R., 56, 60,
    64
Ward, Aaron Montgomery, 47
Washington, Harold, 137, 146
Weed, Thurlow, 3
Weil, Joseph "Yellow Kid,"
    120, 182
Wells, H. G., 42, 129
Wells, Ida B., 188
Wells, Junior, 218

Wentworth, John, 28, 46, 141–42

Whitechapel Club drinking song, 202

Wilde, Oscar, 6, 75

Wilkin, Abra Prentice, 69

Willard, Frances, 176

Wilson, Hack, 98

Winfrey, Oprah, 68, 207, 211, 212

Wood, General Robert E., 59

World's Columbian Exposition, 39–41

Wright, Frank Lloyd, 24

Wright, Richard, 78, 83, 84

Wrigley, Philip, 98

Yates, Sidney, 140

Yeats, William Butler, 13

Yerkes, Charles Tyson, 51

Zuppke, Bob, 108

About the Author

■■■

Chicagoan Richard C. Lindberg, born in 1953, earned a master's degree in history from Northeastern Illinois University. He is the official historian of the Chicago White Sox and the author of many books, including *Chicago by Gaslight: A History of Chicago's Netherworld, 1880–1920* (Academy Chicago) and *Passport's Guide to Ethnic Chicago* (Passport Books). He also served as head writer for the award-winning *Encyclopedia of World Crime.* He is a member of the Society of Midland Authors and the Chicago Crime Commission and serves as the editor of *The Illinois Police & Sheriff's News.*